Moral Stealth

Moral Stealth

How "Correct Behavior" Insinuates Itself into Psychotherapeutic Practice

ARNOLD GOLDBERG

The University of Chicago Press
Chicago and London

Arnold Goldberg, MD, is a training and supervising analyst at the Institute for Psychoanalysis in Chicago, and the Cynthia Oudejans Harris, MD Professor of Psychiatry at Rush University Medical School. He is the author of *The Problem of Perversion; Being of Two Minds: The Vertical Split in Psychoanalysis and Psychotherapy;* and *Misunderstanding Freud.*

The University of Chicago Press, Chicago 60637
The University of Chicago Press, Ltd., London
© 2007 by The University of Chicago
All rights reserved. Published 2007
Printed in the United States of America

16 15 14 13 12 11 10 09 08 07   1 2 3 4 5

ISBN-13: 978-0-226-30120-4 (cloth)
ISBN-10: 0-226-30120-6 (cloth)

Library of Congress Cataloging-in-Publication Data

Goldberg, Arnold, 1929–
    Moral stealth : how "correct behavior" insinuates itself into
psychotherapeutic practice / Arnold Goldberg.
       p. ;   cm.
    Includes bibliographical references and index.
    ISBN-13: 978-0-226-30120-4 (cloth : alk. paper)
    ISBN-10: 0-226-30120-6 (cloth : alk. paper)
    1. Psychotherapists—Professional ethics.   2. Psychotherapist and
patient—Moral and ethical aspects.   3. Interpersonal relations.   I. Title.
II. How "correct behavior" insinuates itself into psychotherapeutic practice.
    [DNLM: 1. Morals.   2. Psychotherapy.   3. Psychoanalysis.
WM 460.5.R3 G618m   2007]
RC480.8.G65   2007
616.89′14—dc22

                                                              2006010710

⊗ The paper used in this publication meets the minimum requirements of the
American National Standard for Information Sciences—Permanence of Paper
for Printed Library Materials, ANSI Z39.48-1992.

CONTENTS

When I write, I do it above all to change myself and not to think the same thing as before. —Foucault 1991, 27

I recently read, in a professional journal, a letter written by a psychiatrist. It told about his and others' experiences of falling in love with and marrying a patient or, in his case, an ex-patient. The letter was offered as a sort of defense or justification of this action. It reminded me of the comments of another psychiatrist, whom I had seen in treatment many years ago, who said that almost all of his friends were ex-patients of his. Both that recollection and the letter made me unhappy. I believe this book is about that unhappy state.

This book is not about or meant to be about correct or incorrect behavior, since I am myself woefully ill-equipped and inadequate to offer a primer or set of guidelines about how to live one's life properly. However, that feeling of mine certainly meant to me that I felt that these two persons had done something that they should not have, that was wrong, but I was not quite able to say just what "wrong" meant. I was unable to be angry with or to feel sorry for them nor, quite surprisingly, to forget about or to forgive them. I could, of course, offer all sorts of psychodynamic explanations for what they had done as well as for how they chose to explain or rationalize their courses of action, along with my own reaction. It was clear to me that they themselves did feel a need to offer some defense or explanation, and this seemed in some way to echo my own discontent.

My personal effort to work out and resolve the sort of discomfort that comes of hearing about any and all forms of moral breaches has led me to various ways to achieve some understanding of how we all respond to the rules and regulations of our practice. What I discovered was a sort of subterranean world of unexamined but powerful directions for living and behaving properly. What I then recognized was that this hidden world needed to be seen in a clearer and more objective way and to be made better sense of. This recognition did not lead to any sort of modification in these directions for correctness, but it did seem to modulate the unsettling feeling that I had in reading that letter. I hope it does the same for the reader who has a similar response to similar news. It may well be a form of therapy.

The case vignettes herein have all been disguised, and some reasons and methods for handling the publication of clinical material are discussed in detail. Since these cases are reports of both psychoanalytic and psychotherapeutic experiences, they may appear not to satisfy the rigors of some psychoanalytic readers or the flexibility of those who practice primarily psychotherapy. However, they are not in any significant way fictionalized.

My thanks to *Psychoanalytic Quarterly* and *International Journal of Psychoanalysis* for their permission to reprint texts. First published in © The Psychoanalytic Quarterly, 2004, *The Psychoanalytic Quarterly*, vol. 73, no. 2, pp. 517–23 ("Who Owns the Countertransference?"); © The Psychoanalytic Quarterly, 2002, *The Psychoanalytic Quarterly*, vol. 71, no. 2, pp. 235–50 ("American Pragmatism and American Psychoanalysis" [published under the title "The Moral Posture of Psychoanalysis and Psychotherapy" in the present volume]); and © The Psychoanalytic Quarterly, 2005, *The Psychoanalytic Quarterly*, vol. 74, no. 1, pp. 253–66 ("I Wish the Hour Were Over"). Chapter 5 is a revised version of an article that appeared in *International Journal of Psychoanalysis* 85, no. 2 (2004): 301–10. Copyright © Institute of Psychoanalysis, London, UK.

I have profited a great deal from discussions about a host of moral and ethical conundrums with my colleagues, friends, and family, and I am sure that any effort to list them all would inadvertently exclude some, so I shall thank them all in absentia. I do, however, owe a special debt of gratitude to my wife, Constance Goldberg; my secretary, Christine Susman; and my dear friend, Bonnie Litowitz.

INTRODUCTION

At a dinner party one evening, an elderly gentleman approached me as I was conversing with a friend and announced that I had, many years ago, been his psychiatrist. As he began talking to both of us my friend drifted away, and I was left alone with my ex-patient as he proceeded to tell me much of what had transpired in his life since we had last spoken as doctor and patient. He was somewhat hard of hearing, so he could hear little of my responses, which themselves were not of much substance, inasmuch as he clearly wanted to dominate this particular exchange. At one point he suggested that we might have lunch together, but I did not respond audibly enough, and the conversation ended with my excusing myself to speak to another person.

I was uncomfortable during that interchange, since it was quite clear to me that I was not at all interested in what he had to say, even though he managed to assure me that the treatment had helped him a great deal. That bit of information was lost amidst a detailed recounting of his present life, which really had no meaning for me. My discomfort was due to both the content of this conversation, as well as to the fact that I was being treated as someone other than who I was. I was no longer his therapist, and I even felt bad that I could not behave as though I were. He, on the other hand, clearly could not distinguish between my present status and that of long ago.

Psychiatrists, psychoanalysts, and psychotherapists of varied and disparate training and background really live in two separate worlds. The world of treatment is delineated by all sorts of behavioral rules and regulations, which are often quite different from those that apply to dinner parties and to the whole of real life. At some times, and for some people, this distinction is clear and unmistakable, as if one were in uniform for one world and in civilian clothes for the other. However, at some times these worlds are collapsed, and we may have the somewhat caricatured picture of the twenty-four-hour-a-day therapist or the less frequent but by no means extinct twenty-four-hour-a-day friendly companion.

It may be felt by many that these two worlds do become one in regard to some issues, especially those that focus on ethics and morality. This assumption—call it the "one-world" assumption—does have some validity in many obvious ways having to do with certain fundamental human values, but there also exist some areas of living in which the life of a therapist and the life of a friend do not at all coincide.

The failure to distinguish between these two worlds, that of the therapist and that of the ordinary human, is not only not at all recognized by some but actually encouraged and championed by others. The thesis to be proposed in what follows is that this failure is a cause of much difficulty, especially in the arena of ethics and morality, two words that have different meanings, as we shall see in what follows.

Until and unless these two different ways of being, that is, therapist and acquaintance, are carefully separated and examined, a certain artificiality may tend to establish itself in the practice of these varied mental health professions, and an equally unnatural claim may be made to differentiate their various procedures from one another. The thesis proposed here is that this problem exists to some degree in all of the above-named practices, and so, with this in mind, they can be considered interchangeably. Thus, this book will not be restricted to psychoanalysis or psychiatry or psychotherapy. We all share this trouble, a trouble that may well be peculiar to these psychological forms of intervention but is also unnoticed by most of us. Hence the word *stealth* in the title.

Although the core problem of the intrusion of the practitioner's character and personality on the conduct and efficacy of the treatment is recognized by most who practice therapy, it has no uniform or agreed-upon way of being dealt with. Psychoanalysis demands a personal analysis, most other disciplines ask for some form of therapy, and almost all require supervision of cases. These forms of regulation, usually for licensing or credentialing purposes, are focused on during the period of training, while the requisite standards for "correct behavior" (as opposed to correct practice) are supposed to be in place for life. It is in the interplay between correct behavior and correct practice, between being what one might call "a good person" and a good therapist, that we are here concerned. In all probability the credentialing demands of the various training programs for therapists do not or perhaps should not turn out "a good person" along with a good therapist. These two goals sometimes coincide but just as well may be quite a distance apart.

The distinction or failure of distinction between these two ways of being is regularly unnoticed except at moments of problematic behavior. It is when an analyst or therapist does something that is clearly marked as "wrong" that we are alerted to what is almost always a failure to distinguish between good practice and good behavior, and it is at these times that we say the two are really one or should be one. On the other hand, it is at times when we feel that a true dilemma exists that we tend to believe that the two are quite separate, that there is no assurance that a good person would do one thing rather than another.

Although a therapist may not really care when listening to a patient tell a tale of woe, it is a given that he or she *should* care. The same is true of all sorts of characteristics and traits and beliefs for therapists in general. The problem arises from the fact that there is no tight fit between the characteristics, traits, and beliefs ideally imputed to therapists and those imputed to nontherapists, who need not care at all. What follows is an effort to disentangle the two lists. It is not at all an effort to dictate whether someone should be one type of person or another. That is an expectation beyond the scope of this book.

PART ONE

The Confrontation between Clinical Practice and Morally Correct Behavior

CHAPTER ONE

Setting the Stage

Paul Ricoeur, the French philosopher, defined *ethics* as "the wish to live well with and for others in just institutions." His is what he called a three-cornered definition, which unites the self, the other, and the third-party bearer in the judicial, social, and political planes (Hahn 1995, 51–52). For Ricoeur, morality concerned itself with the imperatives and prohibitions which thereby regulate ethics. For Ricoeur, ethics was more fundamental than any norm. It could be regulated by more than one set of rules.

Bernard Williams continues this line of thought with his suggestion that morality (the word derives from the Latin) should be understood as "a particular development of the ethical that has a special significance in modern Western culture. It peculiarly emphasizes certain ethical notions rather than others, developing in particular a special notion of obligation, and it has some peculiar presuppositions" (1985, 6). He states that *ethical* is the broad term, whereas *moral* applies to the narrower system. One special concept that belongs to morality is that of moral obligation. Williams says that this moral sense is the outlook of most of us and is directed at what to do in both general and particular situations. Once again, the moral is but one aspect of an overall ethical way to live.

The idea of duty encompassing prohibitions seems to make the moral domain a more useful way to think about the conduct of psychoanalysis and psychotherapy than the much broader field of ethics, which carries with it a good deal of the thinking of religious and philosophical concepts. It is certainly true that much talk about duties and obligations is subsumed under the so-called study of ethics, but a focus on duties, obligations, prohibitions, and imperatives might be better understood under the umbrella of morals and morality.

Morals can be considered as the aggregate of rules under which we live and under which we aim to live well. Living and working under rules and regulations often lend themselves to a set of customs which are taken for granted and may fade into the background. Not surprisingly, they only intrude into awareness at moments of uncertainty or in situations that lack clarity. A psychoanalytic focus on these rules would assign them either to a place in the superego if they are capable of eliciting a feeling of guilt if not properly followed, or else to a less affective experience if they are considered a function of the ego. This will be expanded upon in chapter 11. In the latter case the compromise formation formed by the varied agencies of the mind might well lead to a relative lack of distinctiveness of any such rule. Thus, one might feel that operating as an honest person is accomplished without thinking about it at all. This form of living well is automatic and never an object of self-scrutiny. If, however, it becomes a matter of examination and study, it can be singled out as a true example of a moral imperative. And once it is examined, the psychoanalyst needs to consider what, if any, unconscious determinants have contributed to this once silent but now openly delineated feeling of obligation. However, even beyond the noting of the unconscious contribution to this state, whether capable of producing a feeling of guilt or more comfortably functioning in the ego, there is a need to determine just how it fits in the rest of the personality. Honesty, for instance, may be accompanied by a feeling of pride, while dishonesty may be disavowed and not noticed at all. Thus, a failure to follow a rule, just as much as a submission to one, has a dimension that merits a separate psychoanalytic study. Of course, this form of inquiry should in no way, and by no means, necessarily be in conflict with the more far-reaching ethical considerations, but it may well result in questioning Ricoeur's insistence that ethics is fundamental.

Psychotherapy in comparison to psychoanalysis casts a wider net in its varied ways of functioning and thereby in its wider set of rules and regulations. Some of the suggestions made in the conduct of what is often called psychodynamic psychotherapy in contrast with cognitive-behavioral or other forms of psychotherapy are believed to either stretch or break the rules of psychoanalysis. Indeed, a debate frequently ensues when a suggestion for a particular modification in treatment is made, and the claim is raised that this modification has so broken the rules that it can no longer be called psychoanalysis. Here is an example.

In the words of Lichtenberg and colleagues, "A theory of deficit holds that for the patient to be able to progress developmentally, the analyst gives to the patient what the patient did not get. That is, the analyst 'provides' in response to the need the patient indicates. This provision can be in the form of verbal responses or other new relational expressions" (2002, 177). We shall have occasion later to examine the implications of this form of therapy, but it may be noted here that some argument could be formulated as to whether such "providing" qualifies as a proper technique for psychoanalysis. That, of course, is a definitional question, but it highlights the fact that disciplines and categories are often delineated by their rules and regulations.

If a psychotherapist champions the value of physical contact with a patient, regardless of the efficacy of such an act, it would probably either be classified as a countertransference problem or placed in a category outside analysis. Lichtenberg and colleagues write: "Susan and I held hands, face to face. We sat in silence, feeling the connection. I felt warmth, caring, and affection toward her. . . . Hand holding powerfully communicated that I cared for and valued her, an experience she sorely needed" (2002, 102). Earlier these authors had stated that this was a patient in analysis (p. 101), a characterization with which most analysts would probably take issue. This should serve to demonstrate that breaking the rules that might apply to one sort of activity may be considered perfectly acceptable under a different title. Indeed, jurisdictional disputes are not uncommon in the gray area between psychoanalysis and dynamic psychotherapy, and no agreed-upon referee seems available to settle the argument.

Of course, touching Susan would not in itself be thought of as an ethical or moral breach in most disciplines, but it does fall into the "slippery slope" danger (Gutheil and Gabbard 1993) that is somewhat variable from psychoanalysis to other forms of psychotherapy. At some point in this slope, the consensus imputes a moral mistake. At a certain point, that is, almost all would distinguish between what therapeutic conduct is defensible in terms of efficacy, such as that of touching, and what is morally prohibited, such as sexual intercourse. At times the distinction is made between ethical concerns and technical ones (Dewald and Clark 2001, 102–4), a good example of which might be a case of the analyst falling asleep. For some this is a moral breach, for some a countertransference problem, for some an enactment warranting an inquiry into the patient's participation in the event. The clear difference between the rules and regulations of ethics and the imperatives of morality is often subject to individual choice and preference. Rules are related to procedures, while morals regulate right and wrong.

There may therefore be an alternative position to the one proposed based on technical versus ethical, as in the possible debate between touching and more overt physical intimacy. That stance would insist that there

are only technical actions to be reckoned with, and as long as an intervention works, it warrants a technical acceptance that takes it out of the
ethical domain. This sort of argument could well open the door to a myriad
of actions that would appear questionable or unacceptable to some, but
it highlights the fact that the application and contents of "the moral" are
idiosyncratic and dependent on a multitude of factors.

The idiosyncrasy of the moral system as it enters into psychoanalysis and
psychotherapy is not always recognized as such. Rather, it leads to a variety
of efforts to formulate a simple, standard way of behavior that applies
to every therapist everywhere. This standardization of psychotherapy and
psychoanalysis is in sharp contrast with a position that is more utilitarian,
focusing on the effectiveness of what one does. Perhaps most therapists and
analysts live and work in the space between these poles: one of certainty
about moral correctness and the other of behavior that subserves the desire
to help one's patients. This ambiguous space is the subject matter of the
chapters to follow. The lack of certainty about morals coupled with the
ongoing arguments about proper technique also offers an opportunity to
avoid the entire controversy. That, too, is a call for clarity.

CHAPTER TWO

Positioning Psychoanalysis and Psychotherapy for Moral Concerns

The true injustice is always located at the place from which one blindly posits oneself as just and other as unjust. —Žižek 2004, 79, quoting Adorno

From stem cell research to the experimental cloning of humans, from debates over abortion to the selection of offspring by genetic screening, from sex-change surgery to the casual use of human growth hormone, science is hard-pressed to disentangle itself from moral and ethical issues. Psychoanalysis is an active participant in the debate, inasmuch as it has been variously condemned as an activity intent on undermining morality, as having nothing whatsoever to do with morality, or as itself offering a cogent ethical theory. The first position is represented by Ian Gregory, who says, "Man may achieve a certain guile in pursuing his satisfaction, i.e., he becomes subject to the reality principle, but his end is always the same, his own gratification. He is, in short, wholly self-absorbed, utterly selfish, not capable of forswearing instinctual satisfaction" (1979, 102). Gregory feels that Freud was committed to a narcissistic position that embraced the thesis that everyone pursues his or her own self-interest. Heinz Hartmann (1960) took a slightly different position with his contention that moral evaluations are beyond the analyst's competence and task, and so moral values when they enter into treatment must be accorded the same status as any other facts. Ernest Wallwork is equally convinced that Freud, and so too all psychoanalysis, has a moral psychology that "suggests a social ethic in which the individual is committed to social life, first by an extended egoism in which reasonable social rules are viewed as a long-run practical benefit to the self, and second by an understanding that participation in the community . . . is experienced as a good and pleasure in and of itself" (1991, 29). From one extreme to the other, psychoanalysis is unable to definitively position itself in terms of its ethical status, although this uncertainty is by no means due to a lack of scholarly opinions.

From the perspective of the first group, the practicing analyst would be pursuing an essentially immoral position by encouraging or enabling patients to pursue their own selfish and hedonistic desires. The "guile" that Gregory refers to is but the ego's better way of adapting to the demands of civilization, but that adaptation is in no way to be credited with any sort of altruism. The second group, much supported by many practicing analysts, would sidestep both the accusation and the responsibility of a moral stance. These therapists belong to the "we just work here" contingent and so might claim that analysis may lead to selfish behavior in some patients but may also result in a number of more socially aware and caring persons. This group feels that the process of analysis is not a linear pursuit with a predictable result, and therefore one cannot adopt a particular end point of optimal functioning applicable to everyone. Yet the third perspective challenges this escape from culpability, and insists that morality is built into the system. This last group concludes that there is a mature view on the workings of the pleasure principle so condemned by those who merely stress hedonism. This view takes happiness as the general aim of life, and recognizes that the Freudian position is not a simple one of drive gratification, but a more complex one involving self-scrutiny. Drive sublimation takes into account the demands of society and one's own conscience. Morality here is the very business of psychoanalysis.

The ways that morality and psychoanalysis relate to each other intersect with considerations of theory and practice: is a moral factor applicable to both how one functions as an analyst and how one's own moral proclivities may free or constrain one in theory and in practice? If a particular analyst has firm ideas about how people should or should not behave, it is unlikely that he or she would embrace the first or initial position that espouses selfishness, but it may be equally unlikely that "happiness" would be considered a proper aim for the good life by this or any other analyst or therapist. Indeed, it is one thing to dissect a Freudian take on ethics, as Wallwork (1991) has so eloquently done, and quite another to encompass the variety of personal views about ideal behavior espoused by psychoanalysts, ethicists, and philosophers.

As we move beyond the work of Sigmund Freud to the multitude of post-Freudian contributions, there are, inevitably, additional moral components to the theory and practice as well as to the theoretical positions of the persons involved. Ideas about narcissism that have been developed and put into practice drastically challenge claims about the inherent amorality of psychoanalytic theory. Burgeoning theoretical contributions having to do with countertransference and intersubjectivity barely allow for Hartmann's plea for the objectivity of psychoanalysis. But, perhaps most important, the modifications of psychoanalysis brought about by psychodynamic psychotherapy have forced an examination of the makeup of psychoanalysts and patients alike. We now worry not only about the personality of the therapist but also about what may be best for the wider variety of patients seen in therapy and analysis.

Both positive and negative considerations have an impact on the moral embeddedness of psychoanalysis. One example of the first is the assigning of certain qualities of character to analyst. Stephen Mitchell says,

> We tend not to speak or write much of the analyst's hope as such, because that sounds too personal somehow. The analyst is portrayed as professional, providing a generic service that helps when applied properly. But we all know that it is much more personal than that, that the analyst's hopes for her patient are embedded in and deeply entangled with her own sense of herself, her worth, what she can offer, what she has found more meaningful in her own life. The more we have explored the complexities of countertransference, the more we have come to realize how personal a stake the analyst inevitably has in the proceedings. It is important to be able to help, it makes us anxious when we are prevented from helping or do not know how to help. Our hopes for the patient are inextricably bound with our hopes for ourselves. (1993, 207–8)

This moves a giant step away from the neutral position espoused by Hartmann by introducing the dimension of the analyst's self-worth and his stake in the treatment. We seem to have entered a world that enlarges and makes more central the moral dimensions of psychoanalysis.

Submitting to Morality

A negative aspect of our revised concern with morality is in our preoccupation with boundary crossings and boundary violations. By no means were ethical breaches absent or unknown in the psychoanalysis of Freud's time, but there can be little doubt that they seem to have remained relatively unnoticed or even dismissed in that era. Not so today. We have introduced courses on ethics in psychoanalysis, and we have formed boards and committees to deal with ethical violations. There are extensive guidelines developed as a Code of Ethics by the National Association of Social

Workers and a list of Ethical Principles of Psychologists and a Code of Conduct by the American Psychological Association, along with The Principles of Medical Ethics with Annotations Especially Applicable to Psychiatry by the American Psychiatric Association and in parallel, the American Psychoanalytic Association Principles and Standards of Ethics for Psychoanalysts. These guidelines instruct one on how to behave with respect to issues such as confidentiality and informed consent, as well as on how to handle misbehavior ranging from plagiarism to sexual harassment. In a not so subtle way these guidelines all make it clear that moral issues and moral behaviors have a standing that is overriding and undeniable. Yet as Nietzsche has warned us, "Submission to morality can be slavish or vain or selfish or resigned or obtusely enthusiastic or thoughtless or an act of desperation, like submission to a prince: in itself it is nothing moral" ([1881] 1982, 81). There can be little doubt that the mental health professions compel us to submit to morality. Our ethics casebooks state that their aim is to guide conduct, but typically invoke standards and expectations that are foundational. We are expected to be truthful and responsible, to avoid exploitation, and to protect the public. We have no choice, nor should we. But choice may not be the problem.

The casebook of ethics of the American Psychoanalytic Association carefully lists and describes the standards expected of practicing psychoanalysts and proceeds to illustrate them with ethically demanding situations. The illustrations are engaging and cogent examples, and they merit scrutiny and discussion. They all follow from previously given principles and standards. What seems to be omitted from consideration, however, is what living under these principles and standards does to the analyst and to psychoanalysis. It would seem obvious that submitting to what are essentially a set of preconditions cannot help but have significant effects. The expectation of always being truthful, for example, surely has an impact on anyone who may be more or less truthful but given occasionally to some innocent lying. This not to diminish the virtue of this foundational principle as much as it causes wonder about why we have failed to examine its impact.

One cannot escape this impact if a particular goal is in the mind of the therapist while pursuing a treatment or an analysis. Moving beyond the lifting of repression and making the unconscious conscious, there exists a host of end points that become markedly influenced by the submission to morality. If, for example, we ascribe to Mitchell's conviction that our hopes for our patients are connected to our personal worth along with what we find meaningful in our own lives, then we would necessarily wish to direct our efforts so that our patients' moral standards come close to our own. A dishonest patient would be led along the path of truthfulness by an honest analyst, while a scrupulously honest patient might well be let alone. Since we are not of one mind as to what we attend to in any given patient, a dishonest patient who had few if any qualms about his lack of truthfulness would be seen quite differently by different therapists. However, most issues lie in a gray area of morality, a place of uncertainty. Let us first examine the gray, keeping in mind the yearning we might have for the black and white of knowing exactly how one should behave. The following vignettes can be read as representative of either good or bad practice, and one could readily posit alternate ways of approaching the clinical material. They are not meant as examples of ideal practice but rather those of ordinary practice.

Case Illustration

George came into treatment following his divorce after a long and unhappy marriage. He was the father of three children, about whom he had little positive to say. He had a single younger sister, with whom he had very little contact and toward whom he was bitter due to some family business arrangements in which she felt she was unfairly treated by him. Thus George was angry at his ex-wife, his offspring, his sibling, and both of his parents, who were still alive but estranged from him. In truth, George was estranged from most of the significant figures in his life, and he had little interest in resuming contact with any of them.

In treatment, George lessened his antagonism toward his immediate family, and over time he resumed fairly cordial relations with his parents and sister; but he remained adamant that his now-grown children were ingrates toward whom he had little but negative feeling. Although George professed complete comfort in his decision to extend his divorce from his wife to a similar divorce from his children, his therapist was someone who felt this familial separation was a pathological or at least "unhealthy" one. The therapist theorized that George was unconsciously feeling guilty about not being in contact with his children, and the therapist often found that he wanted to bring the point up for discussion and ultimately to solve this sad situation. Frustrated as he was with the impasse of inducing George to adopt the therapist's own right way to live, he went to a consultant for advice. In presenting his case to the consultant, George's therapist could not and did not conceal his conviction that there was no moral justification at all for George to ignore and neglect his children. As an aside, it was never a matter of financial concern, inasmuch as George had dutifully paid the child support assigned in the divorce settlement along with giving annual gifts to each child according to IRS regulations. The consultant, in contrast with George's therapist, felt that either George was really not at all unconsciously guilty, or else this hypothetical guilt could not be accessed, and so he advised the therapist not to allow his moral standards to intrude on what appeared on the surface to be a relatively successful treatment. George's therapist left the consultation feeling he had chosen the wrong person for advice.

Moral dilemmas do not necessarily lead to happy endings. Nor do they allow for the supposedly scientific stance that regularly betokens a retreat from these dilemmas. Compare the previous statement of Mitchell to that of Sandor Abend, who writes:

> Since I am not convinced of the validity of the reasoning offered in support of proposals to alter the analyst's stance for the purpose of either amelio-rating patients' hypothesized developmental deficits, or of their tendency to misconstrue the analyst's attitude toward them, I prefer another course of action. I think the analyst should pay closer attention to precisely how each patient is experiencing the relationship, and then try to bring the patient's conscious and unconscious ideas about it into their work together. I believe this can be done best by the analyst's maintaining the usual non-judgmental, relatively anonymous analytic posture and attitude, rather than by chang-ing his or her behavior in accordance with preconceived theories about the beneficial impact of such tactics. In fact, I think it is possible that the latter course could sometimes render it more difficult for the analyst to understand that the patient's experience of the impact of the relationship might be quite different from what the analyst hopes to bring about. In any case, it is the patient's subjective experience of the relationship that we seek to understand and clarify, as best we can. (2006, in press)

If George's therapist were to respond to this, he would probably say that the "usual non-judgmental, relatively anonymous analytic posture and attitude" were either a set of fictions or an impossibility, or, even if capable of achievement, an unwise possibility. He simply could not be nonjudgmental, nor did he think that anonymity was called for. He felt it important to communicate the errors of the patient's way, just as he would feel it imperative to be an enemy of dishonesty. In his heart he felt that a nonjudgmental posture and attitude were in themselves a moral standard, because they seemed to say "I care not what you believe or do," which is not at all the same as saying "I will not reveal how I feel about what you do." The first is nonjudgmental, while the second is an artificial device of avoidance. Now on to a more sharply delineated moral quandary.

Case Illustration

Henry was a patient in analysis who routinely loaded up his expense account with all sorts of expenditures of questionable validity. Henry's analyst had for years worked with an accountant who encouraged the analyst to include every conceivable expense on his tax return, including that of paying a salary to his son, when compiling it for IRS submission. Dr. F., the analyst, had not for one moment experienced any concern about following his accountant's advice, since it had always been accompanied by a reassuring "everybody does it" statement of fact. However, when it came to processing Henry's own brand of expense account inflation, Dr. F. had an anxious feeling and an immediate association to his own personal kind of culpability. He tried very hard to maintain an anonymous attitude in response to Henry's wondering out loud about just how Dr. F. felt about his patient's expense account fraud, and his repeated unanswered queries about the state of Dr. F.'s own reckoning with matters of money and responsibility.

Dr. F. thought this was a good problem to take to his own ex-analyst for a combined supervisory session and consultation. He felt that this analyst knew him well and could easily determine just what sort of countertransference problem was hampering his ability to properly handle Henry's hangup. In presenting his case to his ex-analyst, Dr. F. realized that he had always assumed that this relationship had never entailed analytic anonymity, since he was always silently convinced that this rather idealized man was a model of propriety and correctness. Of this he was absolutely convinced, and it turned out absolutely to be the case. His ex-analyst lost no time in concluding that Dr. F.'s problem was not a dilemma at all, but was most likely due to an incomplete analysis of Dr. F. The only solution that he could offer was that Dr. F. return to analysis so that he could do the right thing in his treatment of Henry. His conclusion was based on assuming a parallel blindness of both Henry and Dr. F. in their failing to recognize the nature of their misdeeds. He could not possibly countenance either the dishonest exaggeration of Henry's expense account or the less than honest tax returns of Dr. F. They were on a par as far as this particular consultant was concerned.

Dr. F. was not at all satisfied with this advice from his ex-analyst, and felt he had made a mistake in choosing him for this task. He did not at all wish to return to analysis, nor did he wish to confront his accountant with a newly discovered sense of scrupulosity. All he had wanted was help with a very focused problem, and what he got was a complex set of impossible conditions. Alas, Dr. F. had entered into the arena of moral ambiguity.

As he pondered over the possibilities open to him, Dr. F. could not fail to wonder why his very moral and correct analyst had himself failed to notice the apparent moral delinquencies of his own patient, Dr. F., during the latter's own analytic experience. Would this not also qualify for a certain sort of blindness in that F. had been filing tax returns before, during, and after his analysis? Nor could he easily accept the obvious excuse that the problem had simply never come up in his analysis. Either he was struggling with being honest, or he had no such problem. He tried to imagine what might have transpired if Henry had, instead of going to Dr. F., gone to Dr. F.'s own analyst. The latter might well have quickly attended to this expense account issue with due haste and without any sort of personal anxiety or uncertainty. Dr. F. did not believe that his own analyst would have allowed this material to go unnoticed, nor did he think that this admirable man would have been nonjudgmental. He certainly had been judgmental enough in his hour of consultation. Was it that Dr. F.'s own sort of moral failing was trivial and insignificant, while Henry's was more momentous? Or could it be that sometimes honesty matters and sometimes it does not? Dr. F. effectively disagreed with Stephen Mitchell in that he felt obliged to keep his own sense of personal meaningfulness out of the treatment, but he equally disagreed with Sandor Abend in recognizing the impossibility of remaining nonjudgmental.

Let us consider Dr. F.'s dilemma in terms of considering the three positions outlined above. He could see how analysis certainly allowed one to pursue one's own self-interests in the manner of Ian Gregory, a position that was condemned by some critics of psychoanalysis. But he could also agree with Heinz Hartmann that moral evaluations were simply not the province of analysis, which treated such issues as it would other facts that had no moral connotations. And lastly, he was fundamentally comfortable with Ernest Wallwork's conclusion that psychoanalysis resulted in an individual committed to reasonable social rules. This imaginary thought experiment might also result in Dr. F. finding that he could see going along with Mitchell in that his own sense of what a person should be did impact on his practice. Not surprisingly, he could also go along with Abend in trying to stay as neutral as possible.

Discussion

In the ongoing debate that ranges from stem cells to abortion to genetic screening to the routine use of growth hormones for those of small stature, one dominant voice pleads for a radical disentangling of science from moral and ethical issues. This plea is based on the assumption that the growth and development of science is dependent on an absolute freedom to pursue the goals of scientific inquiry wherever they may lead. Moral positions are inherently constraining and may even alter the direction of scientific pursuits. They have no place in science and only lead to unnecessary problems. We must let science flourish without limits.

The response to this exclusionary position is an equally forceful insistence that ethical considerations can never be removed from scientific activity. One follows rules and regulations because they have developed over time to yield optional results, and returning to ad hoc individual preferences will ultimately lead to various disasters.

Derrida writes: "Every time that something comes to pass or turns out well, every time we placidly apply a good rule to a particular case, to a correctly subsumed example, according to a determinant judgment, the law (perhaps and sometimes) finds itself accounted for, but one can be sure that justice does not." His position is that law is calculable, but justice is incalculable (Derrida 2002, 244). To be just, one must follow the law but also, somewhat paradoxically, suspend it enough to reinvent it in each case. He offers us the theme of undecidability through which every decision must go through in order to be a free decision. He adds, "Once the test and ordeal of the undecidable has passed (if that is possible, but this possibility is not pure, it is never like another possibility; the memory of the undecidability must keep a living trace that forever marks a decision as such) . . . the decision is no longer fully just" (p. 253). To be just, one must not only follow a rule of law but also reinvent it in each case. Each case, each decision, is different and requires an absolutely unique interpretation that no existing coded rule can or ought to guarantee completely. What Derrida terms the "undecidable" remains caught up in every decision. As Slavoj Žižek writes, "The fact that a human subject is constrained in its autonomy, thrown into a pre-given complex situation which remains impenetrable to it and for which it is not fully accountable, is simultaneously the condition of possibility for moral activity" (2004, 76).

These ideas point us in the direction of a strategy that makes use of all the contradictions and uncertainties that we have encountered and will continue to encounter in the chapters to follow. We should entertain the very promising thought that psychoanalysis is a marvelous hybrid that lives by rules that it regularly reinvents. The struggles that George and Henry brought to analysis and therapy are not the kind that are solved by an effort to conform to some standard or principle carried and enforced by the analyst or therapist. Such enforcement of a "law" is too easy. The real solution, one that may make a claim to a just and moral decision, comes about only by living through the painful state of uncertainty. However, this matter becomes more complicated still when we find ourselves looking through the lens of unconsciously embedded guidelines, when we realize we live by words and ideas that are never spoken.

CHAPTER THREE

Moral Stealth

The Problem

When a surgeon scrubs before performing a surgical procedure, one feels that a correct protocol is being followed: a protocol based on well-established principles of asepsis along with a certainty that the neglect of these principles could have unfortunate consequences. Such tried and tested tenets allow no room for discussion or argument, and surely there can be no brief made for surgery without cleanliness. There is a correct, unarguable way to behave. Not so for psychoanalysis and psychotherapy. When a therapist is encouraged or urged or even expected to evince the qualities of curiosity, hope, kindness, courage, honesty, purposefulness, and integrity (Buechler 2004, 9), we cannot possibly consider such expectations as on a par with surgical scrubbing. There is room here for argument. Although one would be hard-pressed to make a claim for successful surgical procedures sans scrubbing, one has little difficulty demonstrating successes in psychoanalysis and psychotherapy with therapists possessed of few or even none of these attributes. We all know good therapists who are bereft of curiosity. Perhaps the outstanding example of the lack of curiosity is seen in those analysts who are confirmed Freudians and who remain closed off to the newer ideas offered by Kohut, Lacan, and others. Indeed, most confirmed believers are susceptible to the death of curiosity. Many of these are fine therapists who might well argue that they have no need to investigate these newer ideas. Curiosity may not be an essential. I personally know of excellent therapists who are not particularly kind, and exceedingly kind therapists who are not much good at what they do. Indeed, there is no tight fit between these perfectly admirable qualities and the proper or even optimum conduct of these psychological treatments. This is not to be taken as a call for the dismissal of this list of what are properly (or perhaps improperly) offered as values; it is to raise the question of how and where the possession of these values became a sine qua non for adequate functioning as a therapist. Surgeons do not have to be kind. Analysts and therapists seem to have no such freedom. Of course, it may be nice to have kind surgeons and kind analysts. But is it necessary?

The Question of Presence

Years ago I read of an experiment conducted by someone whom I felt to be a particularly unkind psychiatrist, an experiment that consisted of having a number of patients speak to a therapist hidden behind an opaque screen. The purpose of the experiment was to determine whether the presence of a therapist was at all necessary for patient involvement and improvement, since the kicker in the set-up was that there was no one behind the screen. The reporting psychiatrist seemed to take great delight in detailing what some of the patients thought about their therapist, and so he was able to conclude that all manner of therapist qualities resided entirely in the patient's head. To the best of my recollection, he did not conclude that therapy sans therapist was a feasible or reasonable road to pursue, but one could not read his report without wondering if it was being offered as a possibility: that no qualities whatsoever were required of a therapist up to and including his or her merely being there. In pondering this implicit, if preposterous, idea I felt the matter of therapist presence is not a matter of kindness but rather of morality. How could one possibly justify having patients speak to blank walls or, better, how could one conduct a practice based on deception? One cannot help but feel the pull toward righteous condemnation of this inherent attitude of depreciation and disregard of another human's dignity, but if this pull is resisted for just a moment, it does allow for another moment of wonder. So let us think about it. Just what does make for analysis and therapy? How do we add up the requirements that take the therapist from presence to competence to expertise? And perhaps we should also wonder how and when all aforementioned supposed clinical values became superadded to these requirements. Is it a fact that some patients get better just by talking to an opaque screen, while others require a collection of qualities that may be beyond some or even most of us? If this is true, it seems quite legitimate to ask how we determine what works for any given person. If it is not true, then it seems essential to find out how we have allowed ourselves to be burdened by a subtle moral message that asks us to be curious, kind, courageous, and so on, and that may well be less than helpful. Once again we must underscore the point that there is no intent here to champion the absence of these qualities as much as to question how and why they have assumed this status of essentials.

Talking to a blank wall differs from talking to a person not only in the qualities and attributes with which we imbue that person, but also even primarily, in the reactions that we receive from the other. Freud's famous effort to hide the analyst's reactions from the scrutiny of his patients by proposing that the analyst become a blank screen fails, not only because of the inability to maintain complete anonymity, but also because muteness can be as powerful a message as a verbal response. The silence of an analyst can never be equated with that of a blank wall, because it is always fraught with meaning until it inevitably becomes part of a ritual that develops a meaning in itself. And so the presence of the other person soon grows into more than a mere site for the projections of the patient. It becomes the study of the relationship that necessarily transcends pointing out the projections of the one and/or gathering up the attributes of the other. What can we make of these relations?

Psychoanalytic Relations

From labor-management relations to foreign relations to object relations, the common note of the series is that of connection. We have a multitude of terms to describe relations, and even within analysis there seem to be different kinds of relations, from the financial to the therapeutic. Initially, it is necessary to determine both what characterizes an analytic view of any sort of relation, as well as what seems especially true of an exclusively analytic relationship. Analysts routinely make comments about (say) a marital relation, and in so doing offer a description of it as seen from the perspective of a psychoanalyst. They do, however, reserve a different and even special place for the analytic relationship, which they tease apart into categories such as therapeutic relationship, working relationship, and at the top of the heap, transference relationship. Thus, for a start we need to differentiate two broad categories of relations: those that have a commonsense description and those whose data are gathered in and by way of psychoanalysis and psychoanalytically oriented therapy. The first may use the vocabulary of psychoanalysis, but only the second is seen as part and parcel of analysis per se. The problem is that the use of the vocabulary of psychoanalysis is often outside the domain of psychoanalysis. If we scrutinize the host of relations that are discussed in analysis, it becomes clear that these two separate categories are not respected as such. Sometimes the mere use of the vocabulary lays claim to belonging to the process. It is only when theory is wedded to technique that we begin to differentiate an analytic relation from nonanalytic relations that may still be discussed from a psychoanalytic perspective.

Buechler (2004, 150) advises us that "in a sense every relationship is a kind of deal," and so she proceeds to describe how those therapists and analysts who compromise integrity in order to preserve the relationship may undermine effective clinical work. Here the quality of integrity assumes the status of an overruling principle. Mitchell (1993) tells us that in the analytic relationship something unconscious is being expressed by and for both patient and analyst, and it can be known only by being lived out in the treatment. Of course, they are both right in their own way, but analytic relationships are not and should not be like "every relationship." And analytic relationships go beyond the mere expression of that something unconscious in that it (that something unconscious) needs to be known. It is relatively easy and obvious to insist on marital relations requiring certain attributes from each partner and/or perhaps desiring other similar qualities in the realm of foreign relations or labor-management relations. However, it may be well beside the point to reduce analytic relationships to any such list of qualities.

First we need to clarify what is different about analytic relationships, and then we need to attempt to determine what is necessary to fulfill them. A definition in the most general sense is in order. It should begin with the nature of psychoanalytic data, which ideally has a status of their own (Goldberg 2004). We then need to ascertain the necessary ingredients or activities that make for improvement or cure in patients. Our definition will state that we gather data of a specific sort in a specific way, and we then utilize these data in some specific manner to effect improvement. Of course, there are any number of qualifications that will embroider any definition, but our interest lies primarily in seeing what is required of an analyst or therapist to proceed in the manner that is outlined; only then can we enlist those principles said to be essentials.

Freud said that analysis aims to make the unconscious conscious and to strive for the goal: "where id was, there shall ego be." This transposition of ideational content was to be carried out by way of its being lived out or experienced in the transference and subsequently interpreted. The data were gathered in the transference, and the interpretation that was offered resulted in conscious knowledge. All that was required of the analyst was to allow the process to proceed and develop without interference. The interference was felt to be due to countertransference arising from the analyst, and so the first spelled-out quality for the success of an analysis which resulted from the analyst's own analysis aimed to reduce and eliminate the countertransference impediment to effective treatment. The analytic relation was framed by this activity conducted within the transference.

Of course, no thumbnail description of the analytic process can do justice to its complexity, but we can still highlight latter addenda to Freud's position that did seem to add more criteria to the qualifications of the analyst or therapist. When Franz Alexander proposed his concept of the "corrective emotional experience" (1958), he, in a somewhat bold manner, asked the analyst to further the transference by carrying on a particular sort of behavior. He did not suggest that analysts adopt a role or exhibit behavior that was not directly correlated with the patient's developmental history. He asked only that the analyst not be the parent of old, and should thereby behave in a corrective manner. He suffered a good deal of criticism for this idea, but much of it may have had to do with the mistaken notion of the analyst assuming an unnatural role.

In stressing the central role of empathy in the data-gathering and therapeutic stance of the analyst, Heinz Kohut seemed to delineate what was expected of an analyst in a way that went well beyond the mere management of transference and countertransference. Kohut was careful and cautious enough to claim that all analysts employed empathy all of the time, and so he was primarily underscoring what Freud had said in other terms. Still there can be little doubt that some analysts took this enjoinder as an attribute of qualification, that is, as something required of the analyst beyond basic competence. Slowly but surely, empathy began to develop a significance that seemed to make it a virtue. Although no one would deny or minimize its value, at times it seemed to serve as a divider between the good guys and the bad guys. And woefully, at times it seemed to be invoked as the singular measure of effective treatment. Compare Alexander's statement, "The discrepancy between the patient's past interpersonal experience, which he repeats in the transference, and the therapeutic situation is accordingly not only due to the objectivity and relative uninvolvement of the therapist, but also to the fact that he is a person in his own right" (1958, 330) to Kohut's claim that the analyst's psychic function is "broken down" and metabolized through internalization processes to become uniquely the patient's own. Only a small additional step is required to Judith Teicholz's conclusion that "the patient's exposure to overt expression of the analyst's distinct subjectivity is inherently facilitative of psychic growth" (2000, 45).

Thus, we see a move from the neutral analyst to the empathic one with a real personality, to the one possessed of qualities that are needed for the patient to grow. This move is correlated with the change in treatment according to different theoretical positions that underline requirements extending from making the unconscious conscious, to developing psychic structure by way of phase-specific empathic disruptions, to more wholesale internalizations of positive parts of an admirable analyst. The blank screen has become a perfect parent (Lomas 1990).

Two Sets of Qualities

Alexander's promotion of the corrective emotional experience was doomed to misunderstanding, because merely being different from the patient's parent failed to account for a presence that was a carrier of all sorts of other qualities. Kohut's emphasis on empathic understanding had to include the component of an analyst who provided for understanding, and inevitably the psychic structure that was formed grew out of the interplay of the patient's and analyst's psychological structures. When one moves on to the relationists and the intersubjectivists, there is no longer any question of the inadequacy of simply making the unconscious conscious. Therapeutic change now seems to depend almost entirely on who the analyst or therapist is.

The explanation offered for this movement in psychoanalysis and psychotherapy is uniformly felt to be one of the necessary growth of our knowledge of what patients need. It was born from learning from our failures and has grown from learning from our successes. This explanation is often qualified by an admission of the need for the analyst or therapist to have an impact that goes beyond understanding and interpretation and so to influence the patient with some of the earlier listed qualities. One is kind to a patient because it both helps the patient as well as allows one to express one's kindness. We do it mainly for the patient but also because, as Alexander said, the analyst "is a person in his own right."

There seems to be a dual set of qualities hidden in Alexander's and others' version of analytic work. The first have to do with what sort of skills the analyst must have in order to properly conduct the treatment. These skills have to do with knowing what to do and say and when to do so. The second have to do with the sort of individual who is doing the job. These latter seem to have more to do with the inevitable impact of the analyst's personality per se on the process. One may or may not be able to tease apart these two sets, but they do appear to belong to different ways that we evaluate therapists. We do tend to say things like "She is a very nice person but seems not to know what she is doing" as well as "He is very smart or good at what he does but is not very nice." We do seem to categorize colleagues in terms of likeability and/or skill. Sometimes these categories seem to be constructed according to affective versus cognitive differences, but so many qualities seem to bridge this divide that once again the result is some form of moral judgment. It sometimes results in the conclusion that good people do good, where the word *good* manages to encompass a virtue along with an ability. Somewhere along the way, the good analyst and therapist was seen to carry an aura of saintliness whereby those qualities of curiosity, hope, kindness, courage, honesty, purposefulness, integrity, and the like became requirements or principles on a par with the need for surgical scrubbing.

Skills and Personal Qualities

If a case were to be made that the personality of the therapist was surely a factor in treating a patient but that it was not crucial in the patient's eventual improvement, then one would have to consider if the move from insight to relation as centrally curative was a move caused by factors other than the therapeutic and subsequently rationalized beyond its significance. The task would be one of considering the categories of technical and social skill requirements and positive personal traits, respectively, to see if there was a valid case to be made for their being crucial factors in treatment, or whether they were products of other forces. One might hypothesize that the increased competition for patients led to therapists who were possessed of certain social skills that allowed them to triumph over their less congenial brothers. With such success, the socially adept therapists may well have done a better job than the socially inept, but the more likely reason would have more to do with public relations and marketing than with competence. It might also be the case that the introduction of psychopharmacologic treatment forced a move to more rapid and cheaper forms of psychologic treatment, and these lesser (for some) forms of treatment were best performed by mental health providers who manifested warmth and kindness more than analytic rigor. There would be no good and easy way to test these hypotheses, since one could hardly design experiments based on these qualities; we are limited to anecdotal data along with a historical study of what is probably best seen as a social experiment.

To recapitulate, there is an ongoing debate that struggles with the sort of personal qualities that contribute to the makeup of the ideal analyst or therapist. These qualities are considered either as allowing a therapist to function best in his or her pursuit of the activity of therapy or else as enabling him or her to be a carrier of qualities that need somehow to be transferred or instilled in the patient. If, for instance, a patient is thought to be in need of a regular pattern of attendance, then a therapist who is reliable and predictable in arranging a schedule of regularity would somehow be felt to impart a positive and possibly curative factor to this patient. Thus, the obvious conclusion is one that espouses a need for a reliable therapist. From this obvious point there follows a host of less clear and ever dubious qualities that extend from honesty to confidentiality to some of the earlier mentioned ones, such as courage. The more controversial qualities seem to go beyond the attributes that one would assign to mere enabling functions such as regularity, and are either regarded as unrealistic by some or resolutely dismissed by others. Kindness seems to be a much desired but perhaps inessential attribute that falls somewhere between a more neutral one, such as regularity, and a more questionable one, such as courage. Perhaps the most arguable quality that gives rise to unending debate is that of love. At one time love was felt only to be a cause for more analysis and so was hardly championed.

The Question of Love as a Necessary Virtue

Peter Lomas writes: "It is certainly the case that a practitioner who consistently writes about love and warmth toward his patients is embarrassing to read. . . . . Yet if it is true that it is in cases where mutual warmth and respect are engendered where the two participants feel love toward each other, that therapy is usually most successful, it would be gravely misleading to omit this fact in order to avoid the charge of immodesty, naivety or sentimentality" (1990, 146). This is a clear example of the move to impute increased efficacy to psychoanalytic and psychotherapeutic efforts that include certain aspects of the practitioner's personality. Of course, there is no evidence other than the anecdotal that the shared loving experience results in more successful therapy, and Lomas's quote seems more akin to special pleading than scientific scrutiny. But Lomas also believes that psychotherapy cannot be divorced from morality, and perhaps his conclusion reflects that belief. In truth, there seem to be as many anecdotal cases of successful treatment delivered by unloving as well as loving therapists, and the ledger seems able to be balanced with *unsuccessful* treatments offered by both loving and unloving therapists. What works well for one therapist may not for another. Most therapists restrict themselves to a narrow spectrum of therapeutic tools, and their successes seem to follow from those patients who do well with those particular tools. A friendly critic might say that Lomas is indeed successful with patients toward whom he feels warmth and respect as well as love, and he is very likely to be unsuccessful with those with whom he is unable to engender these qualities. The likelihood is that he is better able initially to engage with the more fortunate ones, thereby developing a bias in considering who is helped as well as why they are helped. He cannot choose a matching group of unlovable patients to determine the wisdom of his conclusions, and so is convinced of the universality of his experience.

Perhaps somewhere there is a therapist who would claim only difficulty and defeat with patients with whom he felt warmth, respect, and even love, and for whom a respectful distance and even coolness yielded the best results. That therapist wittingly or otherwise chooses to treat patients who best profit from his own peculiar and personal set of therapeutic tools and so may appear at odds with Lomas. Yet each of these therapists may defend his way of practicing, and at some point in the defense there may appear what is essentially a moral or ethical position: a defense based on what not only is effective but also carries a message of the proper way to behave. It may well be difficult for Lomas and this imaginary adversary to separate the ethical and the efficacious, inasmuch as some therapists agree with Lomas that psychotherapy cannot be divorced from the moral. But for some the distinction is clear. For instance, in a recent issue of the *International Journal of Psychoanalysis*, Glen Gabbard (2003) presented a detailed case of a psychiatrist who had committed a boundary violation by engaging in sex with a patient with the explicit motive of it being a therapeutic act. He soon realized the folly of his action, but there was a momentary claim that the sexual intimacy was designed to help the patient. Compare this with Winnicott's (1954) occasional tendency to have patients over for dinner. Each of these escapades might be considered a boundary violation, but one carries a severe moral opprobrium while the other carries an intriguing topic for discussion. You should not do the one, because it is wrong; and you probably should not do the other, because it is unwise. However, the question of the latter's wisdom is left open for many therapists. We seem to make judgments about analytic and therapeutic decisions using a moral compass designed for use elsewhere or perhaps designed for use everywhere.

Discussion

The point is simply that moral positions can have a profound impact on psychoanalytic and psychotherapeutic practice without their being made explicit and often without our ever being aware of them. They have a stealthlike existence and go undetected because of inattention. When one does call attention to what may have a striking valence, especially in terms of an ethical transgression, it tends to be seen solely as an ethical issue. On the other hand, when a relatively harmless departure from the usual forms of practice is made explicit and offered as a reasonable option—such as taking a patient to lunch—it is seen primarily in terms of its therapeutic effect. We seem to switch back and forth between the ethical and the therapeutic without any clear guidelines as to when and how to see something as the one or the other. Some behavior is clear and satisfies the general criteria for misbehavior. However, a host of behaviors lack clarity and can also be rationalized as being in the best interests of the patient. We need less to develop rules of proper behavior and guidelines for correct ethical practice (as important as they surely are) and more to recognize how unspoken and unrecognized moral postures have insinuated themselves in our daily practice. This may be more important than it seems, inasmuch as ultimately everything should be brought under the umbrella of our understanding, whether we like it or not.

In an extensive discussion of a case in which an analyst raised the question of whether or not it is always advisable to avoid physical contact with a patient, Boesky (2005) notes that fully twenty-five authors have weighed in on this case and this rule, with a number taking the side of refusing physical contact and a number promoting or, at least, permitting it. Boesky says that there was a mistaken concern with the rule and a relative neglect of the clinical material, and he carefully avoids taking a position on the rule. A careful reading of his conclusions seems to allow an opening for physical contact and so to move the discussion away from technical con-siderations and over to a deeper scrutiny of the patient's needs. Yet Boesky also claims that "gross boundary violations are always wrong" (p. 849). One is left with a feeling that "gross" may often be an individual decision.

We probably should start off with a recognition that many of our efforts to find a ground for moral judgments put us in an impossible position. Inasmuch as we can never free ourselves from making such judgments, we create what some have called a "condition of impossibility" (Žižek 2004, 76). This, of course, is where a psychoanalyst should properly stand, since our own judgment along with those of the patient and the larger society are all subject to analytic scrutiny. In what may at first seem paradoxical, it is only by our recognition of the impossible situation that we acquire the freedom to make moral judgments. We next turn to the effort to reach judgments by making explicit what is too often implied.

CHAPTER FOUR

The Moral Posture of Psychoanalysis and Psychotherapy: The Case for Moral Ambiguity

Introduction

Probably nothing would be so nonanalytic for a psychoanalyst as assuming the obvious and remaining on the surface, never questioning the evidence as it emerges in the course of therapy. Yet there is probably nothing so accepted, assumed, and defended as the many moral tenets that presently reign in psychoanalysis and other mental health endeavors. There seems to be an agreed-upon and unarguable list of such moral positions as confidentiality, honesty, and respect, coupled with a wish to help and heal, that we readily and even eagerly enlist in the work of all the counseling professions, especially psychoanalysis, without question or worry. That these positions cause us consternation is without doubt; their existence is not.

Keats ([1817] 2001) celebrated the opposite of such sureness with his concept of "negative capability," the state in which one is capable of experiencing uncertainties, mysteries, and doubts without any irritable reaching after fact and reason. Indeed, one might think that the psychoanalytic enterprise should live in this space of uncertainty and tentativeness, but more often than not we are lured by the sirens of rules and regulations and, by means of these directives, of knowing things that are correct and certain. More than mere comfort and safety seem to be involved in such unquestioning attitudes and the associated embracing of absolutes. One should wonder why psychoanalysis of all activities of inquiry would ever be content with buying into foundations; one should likewise rethink whether these foundations really are set in concrete. A twofold problem needs to be questioned here. The first part has to do with the very idea of our going along with positions and concepts that seem without doubt. The second has to do with our unpacking this list of that which is never to be doubted and exposing it to the light of psychoanalytic scrutiny. When we confront the issue of honesty, for example, we regularly insist that the goal of most treatment involves the patient's being honest, to herself and to the therapist. Much less of the inquiry deals with the analyst's own struggle with honesty (Thompson 2004).

The Breach

For the most part we are alerted to moral issues and moral laxity by breaches. When an analyst lies to a patient, our ears perk up. Honesty in and of itself is no call for alarm. We certainly can make no brief here for duplicity, but we know that psychoanalysis is also best served by a reluctance to close the door and to reach finality. One of our favorite maneuvers is to dodge, thereby behaving as if the door had never been opened.

Case Illustration

A potential candidate in psychoanalytic training, in beginning to investigate his possible matriculation, asked his analyst if she were a training analyst, and if so, whether this analysis would qualify in his anticipated application. This particular analyst was herself just beginning to apply to become a training analyst, but since she was just starting the process she truthfully answered her patient in the negative as to his hoped-for status in this analysis, though she qualified her response with the observation that she was on the road to this unique form of certification. Not surprisingly, this patient asked to learn a bit more about the process, and the dutiful analyst proceeded to describe it in some detail, adding that she would be presenting a case to a supervisor, as is required.

Now the wisdom of this revelation is not presently the point, inasmuch as the patient immediately wished to know if he would be the case so selected for this process of inquiry. If we pause at this point, we can probably enlist a number of observers who would advise dodging the question. Surely, some would not have answered at the very start of the questions. Some would inquire of the patient as to his fantasies about the possibility of his role in the process, and some few would have either told the truth or lied. There are a number of possible scenarios here, but not for this particular case.

If this patient was actually the one to be presented for consideration, the analyst was certainly in a bind, especially if honesty is the best policy. Truth may easily take a holiday at this moment, since following it would seem open to a maze of difficulties. Lying would allow for a return to what was probably a more comfortable analytic process. One might argue that this was an unusual event, but there is no doubt that similar such events occur in most long-term therapies, and we are regularly confronted with mishaps in which truth makes for trouble, lies lead to discomfort, and dodging is the best road to relief. That the analyst may have had other options is not here the issue.

One could debate the potential effects of lying to the patient versus telling the truth, but one would probably have to conclude that truth seemed the more virtuous or moral decision and so probably was best for the treatment. But is it not possible that untruth might have served just as well? Without in any way championing a lie, it is surely not self-evident that the treatment works best if one is open and honest. If that were the case, then the popularity of dodging certain painful confrontations would not be so clear. All that one can conclude from this illustration is that a certain moral stance often determines the choices made in the conduct of treatment. And a corollary to this conclusion is that one never questions the efficacy of this stance. Virtue regularly seems to triumph.

One question that may be considered self-evident and thus unnecessary to posit is what the requirement of a set of moral standards means to an analyst and to an analysis. It is rather routinely assumed that the man or woman of virtue is by definition the ideal person to conduct a treatment, but surely that assumption could and should be examined even if it is not to be too readily called into question. More to the point is questioning just what unconscious factors may result in such a desirable final product. Is the analyst who is honest, maintains confidentiality, never abuses a patient, respects privacy, and has the patient's best interests at heart a person whom we all should aim to become? Or is it possible that the construction of such an ideal carries problems of its own? We all agree that therapists and analysts are not equally possessed of such virtues, but all seem to agree also that we should approximate the ideal as closely as possible.

Examining the Virtues

If we concentrate on just a few of the virtues expected of an analyst, we may necessarily overlook others; perhaps instead we may generalize about both their essential need as well as the impact of these requirements on the practicing analyst.

Case Illustration

A published case (Harvard Ethics Consortium 2003) was presented to readers as an ethical dilemma. Although a patient had earlier given his permission for publication of his treatment, when he finally did see it he became upset and was forced to briefly return to his psychiatrist in order to hash out what he felt were mistakes and surprises in the written account. He also published a piece in the same journal to explain his reactions. The assembled ethicists were of one mind; that is, the patient must be given primary consideration and so be protected from injury by poorly disguised or recognizable clinical material. The therapist was reluctant to fully share his feelings about the patient during the treatment, because he felt it would be hurtful to the patient to do so. Some might feel that a treatment can only be effective if a therapist is completely open, while others might counsel judiciousness in this regard. One must protect the patient from being recognized or embarrassed or hurt. Suffice it to say that it seemed that the therapist was faced with a Hobson's choice: either not write about the patient at all or attempt a variety of maneuvers, all of which carry a risk that may lead to a condemnation readily offered by ethical experts.

The advice given to those who would write and publish clinical material is that of choosing one or more of a variety of maneuvers to protect a patient's privacy. These range from disguise, to collaboration with the patient, to having the contribution be an anonymous one, to writing about process with no revealing data, on to the construction of a fictionalized encounter. The scholars who write about these maneuvers all agree that none of them are foolproof, and one always runs a risk of recognition (Galatzer-Levy 2003). Thus, the caveat to any advice is the need to aim for a fit between our attempt at concealment and patient protection and what might best apply to a particular patient. There is no single rule to follow. If one writes, one must take risks and face the consequences. Writing can be avoided entirely, while other moral imperatives, such as honesty, are ever with us. One might be well advised to avoid the whole process, as no doubt many do. I shall revisit this case from a different perspective in chapter 9.

Clinical writing does appear to involve factors beyond the consideration of honesty, inasmuch as there is in writing a clearer set of opposing forces that seem to have equal rights, that is, protecting the patient and communicating ideas. On the other hand, to tell the truth or to lie is a choice that we feel we are not to struggle over, since the choice would seem obvious. Clinical writing involving the description of a patient is seen as desirable only as long as it is done with the patient's interest in mind. We are expected to balance the choices. If we review the list of moral and ethical constraints visited upon a psychoanalytic or psychotherapeutic practice, we see that they range from the fairly easy to the unbelievably complex. However, we may also see that what is easy for one person may be complex for another. What would seem to be obvious—do not lie to a patient—turns out to be a quandary for some. What would appear to be desirable—to share one's knowledge with the scientific community—turns out to be a potential obstacle course. Do we need to turn to ethicists to resolve these dilemmas, or can our problems remain within, and be handled, by our own methodology? First, let us see what, in the most general sense, the study of ethics has to say. For the most part, I shall initially steer clear of religious positions, which seem to join with or buttress the ethical ones.

Ethical Answers

Moral philosophers from Socrates to Jesus to Kant to Rawls have offered guidance and directions on how to live and what constitutes the good life. Socrates felt that the good life is also the life of a good person. Religion, or better, perennial philosophy (Flanagan 1996), says that there is an objective moral truth, a right way to think and to behave, and this is divinely communicated to people. John Stuart Mill and Immanuel Kant each proposed a secular ethical theory that comes close to that proposed by Jesus. I cannot begin to develop here the ideas proposed by the moral philosophers, but merely to underline that they present moral issues as both foundational and universal, whether from divine guidance or from the obligations imposed on us by our humanity. Indeed, Emmanuel Levinas (2001) claims that ethics arise in relation to the other and not from a law; he insists that the relation to the other person imposes a responsibility for one's very being.

Michael Oakeshott stands in contrast with the moral philosophers by writing:

> A morality is neither a system of general principles nor a code of rules, but a vernacular language. General principles and even rules may be elicited from it, but (like other languages) it is not the creation of grammarians; it is made by speakers. What has to be learned in a moral education is not a theorem such as that good conduct is acting fairly or being charitable, nor is it a rule such as "always telling the truth," but how to speak the language intelligently.... It is not a device for formulating judgments about conduct or for

solving so-called moral problems, but a practice in terms of what to think, to choose, to act, and to utter. (1975, 78–79)

He says we should think of morality not as the voice of the divine part of ourselves but rather as the voice of ourselves as members of a community.

Richard Rorty says that looking at morality as a set of practices makes it the voice of a contingent human artifact subject to the vicissitudes of time and chance (1989, 60). Here we approach an alternative view to the foundational, a view offered by Owen Flanagan, who states that "morality resists theoretical unification under either a set of special-purpose rules or a single general-purpose rule or principle, such as the categorical imperative or the principle of utility. If this is right, and if it is right because the ends of moral life are plural and heterogeneous in kind and because our practices of moral education rightly reflect this, then we have some greater purchase on why the project of finding a single theoretically satisfying moral theory has failed" (1996, 127). Flanagan's alternate or nonfoundational stance invites a critical examination of the possible heterogeneity of the moral standards for life, especially those that so dominate the practice of psychoanalysis and psychotherapy.

We Would Be Like Gods

What is it about being a psychoanalyst or a psychotherapist that may lead to such a strict and often unwavering posture of moral rectitude? Hand in hand with that question goes the corollary: why do we not analyze this posture instead of embracing it? This peculiarity is not in our practice in dealing with patients. Faced with the psychoanalytic inquiry into the moral certitude in our patients, we might wonder about the state of a superego that was so rigid and unyielding, and we would question the origins of this psychic state. An investigation would follow of the psychological origin and concepts of an ideal that seemed to insist on an almost godlike stance of virtue and wholesomeness.

In chapter 5 I shall examine the universality of confidentiality as "a basic patient right and an essential condition for effective psychoanalytic treatment and research" (Dewald and Clark 2001, 21). My hope is to soften this absolute insistence on confidentiality as an essential right in our field. No opposing position of free and open exchange of patient information is put forth, but rather the question of its being a necessary and essential condition for treatment is raised. It likewise seems both appropriate and necessary to examine what this requirement demands of a therapist. He or she is asked never to reveal anything that is said about pretty much anything and everything. Secrecy and privacy are the watchwords. One is even enjoined from telling a third person some noncritical gossip or information heard from a patient, lest it somehow get back to the patient that the therapist is indiscreet. We are regularly advised that we cannot behave like ordinary people but rather must be a bit extraordinary. Susan Wolfe, a philosopher, describes what she claims is a life of moral sainthood, a life that may be a clue to an analogous therapeutic sainthood:

> A moral saint must have and cultivate those qualities which are apt to allow him to treat others as justly and kindly as possible. He will have the standard moral virtues to a nonstandard degree. He will be patient, considerate, even-tempered, hospitable, charitable in thought as well as deed. He will be very reluctant to make negative judgments of other people. He will be careful not to favor some people over others on the basis of properties they could not help but have. (1982, 421)

Compare this description to that offered by Edelstein, who considers the central values of psychiatrists as including "beneficence, altruism, respect for persons, respect for autonomy, nonmaleficence, clinical competency, fidelity, integrity, confidentiality, veracity, justice, and respect for the law" (2005, 10).

These perfectly reasonable and desirable qualities may also be seen as burdensome. Wolf thinks that the moral virtues are apt to crowd out the nonmoral ones and indeed may be incompatible with a desirable personal life. At a conference someone told a vignette that had to do with a patient telling him that John and Mary were planning to marry. As luck would have it, he soon after ran into John, who approached him and happily announced, "Did you hear that I am going to marry Mary?" What to do? Rather than openly and happily acknowledging this bit of information, he was forced to dodge or lie or utilize some maneuver designed to conceal that he had learned of this from a patient. Of course, one may devise other options for handling the situation, but a straightforward yes is often far down on the list.

There is no argument as to the wisdom of the probable concealment. Rather, it is open to investigation as to what this somewhat unreal way of behaving asks of us and does to us. Flanagan (1996, 190) says that we develop many traits for what are clearly nonmoral reasons, and some may necessarily obstruct satisfying our ideals of moral sainthood. For example, one could imagine a conception of morality that is so demanding that it precludes the development of certain traits and talents and prevents the undertaking of projects that are desirable. If we return to the vignette of the analyst who was ambitious enough to wish to become a training analyst, she could well have avoided her momentary moral conflict had she somehow managed to squelch this ambition to become a training analyst. Again, this is meant to be only illustrative, not prescriptive, in the hope of directing our attention to the continual and perhaps unnecessary moral constraints that we have often unwittingly adopted.

The wholesale embrace of moral sainthood may be a caricature, but it seems to have its origin in an implicit agreement between patient and analyst that the former is naïve and innocent and the latter is omniscient and omnipotent. Although our literature is replete with incidents of boundary crossings and boundary violations, one is strained to read or hear of cases where episodes of moral righteousness were analyzed. Surely, this adoption of a role of unwavering honesty, confidentiality, helpfulness, complete absence of any wish to exploit or abuse, and whatever else one wishes to add to the list of therapeutic virtues is just as plausibly an instance of countertransference as the failures to evince these virtues.

Admitting to Self-Indulgence

We are not all selfless and saintly. We charge patients, we adjust our schedules in order to maintain some level of personal comfort, we gossip a bit or a lot, we are often jealous and competitive, we tell little or big lies, et cetera, et cetera. We are human. The single most distinctive attribute that should differentiate analysts from nonanalysts is that they employ the instrument of analysis. The same, of course, applies to all therapists in an analogous manner, inasmuch as our personal self-reflection on what we do must be the sine qua non of how we differ from nontherapists. This should be an example of how our everyday nonmoral action at times overrides what seems to reflect the ideals of moral sainthood. Our humanity contradicts the Socratic position that it is good to be good.

Case Illustration

Dr. S. was startled to receive a letter from his local ethics committee that a complaint had been filed against him. The letter revealed only the name of the complainant with no clear reference to the infraction. The name was that of a patient who had terminated some time earlier in order to take a position in another country. Dr. S. felt this was a premature termination but felt a good deal had been accomplished, and so was surprised to read of his ex-patient's unhappiness and dissatisfaction. When Dr. S. did get to read the full complaint, it was directed at the patient's having heard that his case had been presented at a clinical conference, and in the presentation a specific interaction between analyst and patient was quite clearly about him. The patient was incensed that he had not been asked to give permission for the use of this case material, and so complained that this presentation might well lead to various persons learning about the fact that he was in treatment, and that this particular interaction was about him. Of course, he would never have given such permission, and so he initiated this complaint. The patient was a mental health professional, and so claimed that he had cause to worry that there was a modicum of likelihood that these revelations would result in professional embarrassment.

At the ethics hearing that followed, Dr. S. said that the patient was adequately disguised. The patient responded that his own ability to recognize himself made it possible that others would as well. As a matter of fact, no one did, but that seemed not to move either the patient or the ethics committee. After a good deal of discussion, the assembled peers decided merely to warn Dr. S. to take more care in the future. In this practical sense, he was mightily relieved, but in another sense he was quite troubled, because he felt that this relatively mild chastisement was misdirected. He mulled over the anger that the patient still lived with and could not help but feel that the disillusionment and disappointment stemmed from issues that the patient had with his father, and that had not been properly analyzed. Dr. S. was convinced that he was at fault, not for a moral breach but for a blindness to his own need to be well regarded. As in so many ethics hearings, what was played out was a psychotherapeutic mishap rather than an inquiry into a moral digression. Dr. S. could rationalize this sad incident by the fact of the patient's premature departure from treatment. We can never know if that explanation also was a result of his lack of recognition of his own need to be seen as flawless. Narcissistic preoccupation with personal perfection can reveal itself in a myriad of ways, ranging all the way from presenting one's cases to gratify an exhibitionistic need for recognition to never presenting one's cases in response to a need for the comfort of moral rectitude.

Case Illustration

In sharp contrast with the above example of Dr. S. was an experience of Dr. D., who gave a clinical presentation which omitted a case that was both cogent and relevant but that Dr. D. felt was not to be openly discussed, because the patient was a mental health professional. Much to Dr. D.'s surprise and amazement, his patient asked in a very matter-of-fact manner just why his own case had not been a part of the presentation, since it seemed to represent exactly what had been the point of the paper. Initially, Dr. D. took this question and implied request of the patient to be a derivative of a grandiose wish to be the center of attention, but Dr. D. could only offer, in his supposed defense, a wish to protect his patient. The patient quickly responded that he had no need for such protection, had not ever asked for such protection, and in fact had never felt that a disguised case presentation would in any way make him vulnerable. Once again Dr. D. tried to explain as best he could what he had done or, in this instance, not done, but he inevitably seemed to end up with some variant of "the doctor knows best." He quite reluctantly realized that this final redoubt was designed primarily for comfort within the walls of an assumed moral perfection allied with a reluctance to take a risk. Dr. D. allowed himself what he later came to realize was an unusual period of self-reflection, one that was directed to the question of just why he had felt it necessary to be such a good and thoughtful therapist. This was unusual, because he could not remember any previous self-analysis about why he felt so pleased with being such a good boy.

Discussion

Emmanuel Levinas, the French philosopher who has great suspicion about the practice of psychoanalysis and its abuses (2001, 118), claims that the ethical relations of which he speaks are a lived mental experience not further reducible. Aside from his general lack of knowledge about psychoanalysis, he has effectively ended the conversation. Yet his is a powerful voice that places the foundations of all of our relations with one another beyond inquiry, even, in his words, considering them primordial. In a similar vein, any psychoanalyst who has studied religion and its place in psychology is able to distinguish an individual's needs and desires and beliefs about religion from the individual's faith. The latter is felt to be incontestable and akin to a gift. One cannot ever take a stand "for" or "against" faith, but one can mount an inquiry about what the presence or absence of faith may mean for a particular individual. So our examination of what our moral postures do for our practice of psychoanalysis will get no help from Levinas, nor should we expect it to, since he begins from a place that obviates our inquiry. He is, however, an unwitting foil to use as representative of the many voices of certainty and the accompanying foundation from which all decisions can be adjudicated. Thus, we shall have further occasion to consider his positions.

Of course, one may feel free to analyze the unconscious need of Levinas to reach for something primordial and fundamental, but that by no means allows its dismissal any more than his own dismissal of psychoanalysis is warranted. So the role of religion in the study of moral certitude in psychoanalysis is best put to the side. We put it to the side because of its inherent wish to be overriding. This wish inevitably leads to conflict, since psychology has its own wish to be overriding. The views are incommensurable. We best stay with psychology.

I wish to make a case for moral ambiguity. We often should and do find ourselves in situations in which we lack confidence that we have done the right thing (Flanagan 1996, 132). A natural tension exists among the pressures to do right in the sense of a greater community or society, to act correctly vis a vis another human being, and to satisfy one's own values and sense of right. These pressures rarely yield simple answers but rather allow for a plurality of possibilities. There is no single right way to think, live, and be. This sort of moral relativism, easily dismissible by many, provides an opportunity to see if its prevalence has forced psychoanalysis erroneously to embrace some sort of absolute position that allows us to take false comfort in having done the right thing.

Psychoanalysis has something to offer the state of moral ambiguity, and so needs to foster the experience of not knowing too quickly if we have or have not done the right thing. In fact, ambivalence and uncertainty are hallmarks of the psychoanalytic enterprise. When we see a patient struggling with indecision, we do not see it as a time to take sides with one position or the other. When we see a person who is stubbornly fixed on one position with no awareness or allowance for opposing points of view, we often conclude that an internal conflict is being solved by this extreme of certainty. Although there is no automatic way to ascertain what is the source of either the struggle with ambivalence or the embrace of a certain conviction, each signals an invitation and a requirement. And the invitation and requirement are not restricted to the analytic or therapeutic study of our patients. We must resist these psychological resting places in ourselves. Our self-analysis should be the guide that allows us to continue not knowing if we have done the right thing. We operate in a network of self-correcting attitudes and actions, and this naturally leads to a multitude of possible results. Recognizing this potential pluralism may be a healthy antidote to the unconscious need that many of us have to aspire to a version of moral perfection. It is a sobering and healthy idea to realize that other ways of doing things may be just as "good" as our own.

Summary and Conclusions

There is now and to some degree has always been a great deal of attention paid to issues of misbehavior, of boundary crossings and boundary violations, in the practice of psychotherapy and psychoanalysis. Some of this attention has carried a certain moral fervor as an accompaniment, and this fervor often is delivered as an absolutarian position that tolerates no dissent. If we were, as analysts, to see such fervor in either a patient or a politician, we might well consider the possibility that an opposing impulse was operating elsewhere.

This is not a brief for moral laxity. To urge that we examine our moral posture is not ever to suggest that we abandon it. Rather, it is a plea for pragmatism in the practice of psychoanalysis and psychoanalytic psychotherapy. Let me be clear just what I mean by pragmatism. It is not the same as relativism, which suggests that any idea is as good as any other. Rather, it is a stance that claims that there are no constraints on inquiry (Rorty 1982), there are no absolute guiding truths save those we gain from conversations with one another. From such conversations we may well decide on absolute positions such as forbidding cruelty and the sexual exploitation of patients. However, other moral positions that pertain to confidentiality, clinical presentations, and even honesty may lead to a more relative position. Pragmatism is not the defense that we do what works, as might be championed by those authors who hold hands with and regularly love their patients, but is an invitation to continue the conversation, with the implicit recognition that we shall probably never arrive at the truth for all time.

The intellectual history of pragmatism began in the early 1900s, with William James, Charles Peirce, and John Dewey. Each of these men warrants a lengthy historical exposition of his life and ideas, but all of them might well agree upon the essential idea of pragmatism: "Thought is an integral and constitutive part of historical experience. Truth is something that happens to an idea within the exigencies of a particular time and place" (Pettegrew 2000, 3).

Pragmatists state that knowledge does not coincide with the correspondence of facts and sentences, but rather that the participants in communication agree upon a shared interpretive horizon. One can readily see dangers lurking in the proposal that we do not correctly perceive the world, but instead gather about us a group of people who agree with us. We do not collect facts in order to obtain truth and knowledge that will be good for all time, but rather we hold a medley of workable opinions. Our thinking is not a record of representations of the real world, but a series of more or less successful operations upon the world.

Acceptance of such statements may very well cause us to abandon fundamental or foundational beliefs about the world in order to join with the pragmatic rebels. This movement away from a philosophy of certainty or positivism is, not surprisingly, just what has been happening to a large extent in American psychoanalysis. Unfortunately, this change in analysis has not been seen and studied as part of a historical process, but has instead been criticized as evidence of disloyalty to Freud and to classical analysis, as reflective of mistaken ideas about science, and (most unfortunately) as simply bad philosophy.

To paraphrase the pragmatists and apply their philosophy to psychoanalysis, if there is "no way the world is," is it also true that "there is no way a patient is"? This question has been seen as a consequence of Nietzsche's perspectivism (Allen 2000, 141), which seems to say that your view (or guess) is as good as mine. Pragmatists argue that consensus and only consensus is the governing rule for what is right and correct. They refer to what is most useful as being most justified, and therefore, they insist that it is *what accomplishes such an end point* that becomes the bearer of the way the world is.

If there is no way the world is and no way a patient is, then it may readily follow that there is no single way to either react upon the world or properly treat a patient. If what works becomes the guiding light for therapeutic intervention—as it does for the activity of just about any accomplishment espoused by pragmatists—then one need not evaluate therapeutic behavior against a background of a set of correct or prescribed rules and regulations. Rather, one practices with an eye both to the chosen activity being effective *and* to the maintenance of a consensus of like-minded persons who constitute a community of support. Only then can we claim validity for what we do.

It is surely at this point that many people part company with pragmatism (along with the more denigrated relativism and postmodernism), inasmuch as they begin to feel that the ground is going out from under them, along with the set of personal beliefs and principles of personal training by which they have lived (and even prospered).

The parallel between pragmatism and psychoanalysis requires that we describe the present state of the one along with that of the other. One way to sum up pragmatism is to see it as a form of naturalism, or simply the way human beings cope with the world. To sum up much of today's psycho-analysis, we might describe it, too, as the variety of ways analysts cope with the problems of their patients. Of course, at each and every presentation of one or another method of such coping, a critical eye may determine that this or that is no longer qualified to be considered a proper component of the analytic community. And so at each and every presentation of a particular method, the effectiveness of the treatment may take a backseat to the issue of credentials, that is, remaining within a tradition.

In addressing psychoanalysis, pragmatism would ask that we recognize that we are engaged in conversations aimed at increasing our capacities to better make our way in the world. Each of these conversations employs a favored vocabulary. Only the test of effectiveness should cause us to choose one over another. And effectiveness is always relevant to time, place, and consensus.

Although there may be a good deal of disagreement, it does seem to be the case that differing schools of psychoanalysis help many people, and they seem to do so in roughly equal numbers. To be sure, one particular patient may not profit at all from one approach while doing quite well in another, but no school of treatment is a complete bust or can claim one-hundred-percent effectiveness. They all work. None can trumpet its superiority over the other based on a track record of cure or improvement or patient appreciation. We presently have no comparable statistics, so we rely on folklore. Therefore, the relevant question is why and how such diverse, and even oppositional, ways of practice can enjoy relatively equal effectiveness.

Unfortunately, that question is usually either dismissed or not even asked. The preferred question we typically hear is how so many thoroughly erroneous or wrong-headed approaches have managed to fool so many people! There is a good deal of attention paid to issues of deviance or difference rather than to those of consensus. We tend to listen to others while marshaling an argument, rather than being open to what may be beneficial for a particular patient.

American pragmatism would make the claim that today's psychoanalysis is continually asking the wrong questions, because it is consumed by the myths of our ability to gain and represent certain knowledge. We argue over who is right and who is wrong, who is loyal and who is unfaithful, and who can wear the banner of certitude. As long as we accept the dualism of subject versus object as a reality, we shall labor mightily over whether the patient's ideas have somehow found a home in our minds and managed to take over our thoughts. As long as we believe in the world of facsimiles of persons populating our minds, we shall worry over whether these representations have become better or worse organized, more split or more whole, and, especially, closer to looking like we would like them to look. And as long as we know what is best for our patients, what is the right way to live and think, we shall be able to make a claim as to whether the patient has finally gotten it right. The pragmatist would ask that we work at doing without these fundamentals and foundations; he or she does not say that these fixed positions are wrong so much as that they limit one's freedom.

I believe the pragmatist would also ask us to change our question about the mistakes of other schools to one that asks what each does that works. Our hope for this commonality of inquiry should be directed toward an appreciation of the effectiveness of diversity. Somehow, somewhere, we must all be doing something right. That rightness cannot be dismissed as suggestion or transference cure or just plain luck, although all of those factors may also be operant. There is more to it than that, and our preoccupation with differences has blinded us to whatever it may be.

Someone might say that the practice of psychoanalysis and psychotherapy by its very focus on healing and its central theme of empathy is by definition a moral undertaking, and so its moral posture grows out of this fundamental conception of what we do. There is no doubt that this is true for some people some of the time. But once again we must recognize the operation of a pragmatic principle in our work as well. One need not and cannot override the other. That is the problem with moral imperfection, and it is also our happy fate.

Thus far we have noted that the proper conduct of psychoanalysis and psychotherapy is often said to be guided by a set of technical procedures, some of which in turn are constrained by a number of rules and regulations. These rules are an amalgam of ethical procedures which we term moral imperatives, plus a quite differing collection of human qualities which, for some therapists, lay claim to the status of necessary additives to the technical procedures. One result of this combination of procedures, constraints, and qualities is a lack of clarity and/or an inherent ambiguity. Another result is the fading into the background of one or two elements of this triad, of technique, rules, and personal characteristics required for proper therapeutic results. Together we confront both moral ambiguity and moral stealth. Next we shall investigate how a turn to certainty poses still further problems. Some moral imperatives that are not to be challenged may turn out to be antithetical to good practice.

PART TWO

Difficulties in Reconciling Correct Behavior with Psychoanalytic and Psychotherapeutic Practice

CHAPTER FIVE

A Risk of Confidentiality

Introduction

The idea of a "background" is prominent in certain philosophical circles (Searle 1992), but it is often a rather elusive idea to define. It has to do with the tacit assumptions or things taken for granted in any situation, from a social gathering to a workplace. These assumptions are said to be both basic and not in need of attention. For instance, such a background operates when we go to a restaurant and assume that there will be a menu, that we can purchase food, and that a bill will be offered to us: all things that need not be spoken of overtly. We can imagine such a set of assumptions in many other normal situations, and it takes no stretch of our imaginations to see how it may apply to psychoanalysis and psychotherapy. Over time the ordinary and accustomed ways in which we as analysts and therapists operate become so routinized that they fade into the background and are no longer subject to concern and attention. With such comfort and convenience, a certain risk may become operative.

In the previous chapter, I discussed how the development of the rules of psychotherapy and psychoanalysis has led to moral commitment to their adherence. Such a commitment tends to give these (often implicit) rules a certain air of absoluteness which may, in turn, detract us from analyzing them. Rather than our becoming alert to every nuance of analysis, we allow our routine to fade into the background. This background may at times impede the practice of these disciplines.

There should be little doubt that many if not all of the tried and true principles of psychotherapy or psychoanalysis may benefit from being subjected to periodic reexamination to see if their status remains as relevant to today as they did when first developed. This reevaluation has been brought to bear on such issues as frequency of visits, the use of the couch, self-disclosure, and so on, and, more often than not, it has led to confusion and debate rather than to certainty and closure. This unhappy end point would, however, appear to be quite unlikely with an issue such as confidentiality, an issue claimed to be "a basic patient's right and an essential condition for effective psychoanalytic treatment and research," as stated in the *Ethics Case Book of the American Psychoanalytic Association* (Dewald and Clark 2001). This particular casebook is meant to serve as a guidebook of general principles. It presents a series of potential problems for all sorts of ethical dilemmas. Those concerning confidentiality offer enough exceptions to the aforementioned basic right to confidentiality to cause consternation for any psychoanalyst or psychotherapist. I will develop the idea of the fading of ideas into the background, utilizing the assumption of a basic right of confidentiality. My aim is to demonstrate that this basic belief has allowed us to fall back on an absolutist position. This position carries a risk of its own, while its relativistic counterpart is equally problematic. Of course, avoidance of any moral position whatsoever may hide its own authoritarianism.

The exceptions to the maintenance of confidentiality in psychoanalysis range from supervision, if the patient is disguised, to insurance reports, to communication to lawyers and courts, to talks with family members, and on to publications in professional journals and the lay press. These exceptions are all defensible and desirable. One immediate response to this plethora of possible breaches in confidentiality is a conviction that there are no easy answers. Yet another response is admirably presented in a book by Bollas and Sundelsen, who offer a compelling case to support the claim that "a patient who sees a psychoanalyst is guaranteed that absolute confidentiality is assured and maintained, (and) then the door is shut to any and all requests from third parties for clinical notes and testimony by the clinician" (1995, 155). The single exception allowed by the authors is for consultation with a supervisor, with the patient remaining anonymous. That exception is allowed for the benefit of the patient alone.

In order to handle the inevitable pressures brought upon a therapist for breaks in this absolute position, Bollas and Sundelsen offer the position of "social therapist" as one (in sharp contrast with a psychoanalyst) who both treats the patient and actively intervenes in the patient's life. The authors insist that one cannot practice psychoanalysis with the basic premise of free association if one does indeed step outside this fundamental rule, and they bemoan the sad state of much of today's analysis, which seems to routinely betray such an absolute condition. Such betrayals, other than consultations, are seen as effected for the benefit of third parties.

An Outline of the Problem

If one were to list the rather ordinary requests and demands for breaks in confidentiality, they would fall into two categories. The first would have to do with those which would benefit the treatment, and the second with those which would benefit others but may either harm or benefit the treatment. For Bollas and Sundelsen, the first category would have but one entry: that of consultation with a colleague or supervisor, with an adequate disguise of the patient. For many others, as described in the *Ethics Case Book*, there is a host of situations which do ultimately benefit the patient, such as informing insurance companies, albeit at a price. For the most part the second category is filled with benefits for others, with an undetermined harm to the patient. The absolutarian standard of Bollas and Sundelsen is both reassuring and comfortable. But one should wonder. In a very telling quote from a psychoanalyst who struggled with a law prohibiting psychiatrists from testifying without a patient's permission, we read: "This honorable attempt to protect the patient misses the essential point that he (the patient) may not be aware of unconscious motives impelling him to give permission." One might also change that quote to end with "to conceal information." And one may extend that dilemma to include the psychiatrist in the exchange. Without in any way diminishing the passion and point of the absolute stance on confidentiality, one should surely wonder if such a stance also serves to bypass unconscious motives in the therapist in the guise of a noble pursuit.

A very touching incident is described by Romulo Lander, who wishes to demonstrate the tensions and emotions that might cause an analyst to, in his words, "break confidentiality." Lander feels that analysts should "occupy a place of privileged listening without exercising value judgments." By utilizing a particular theoretical outlook involving working either in symmetry or asymmetry which he attributes to Lacan, Lander explains how the analyst oscillates between identification with the analysand and maintaining free-floating attention. He notes that the loneliness of the analyst at times puts her into a symmetrical relationship, which may lead to her being "incapable of continence" and so to breaking confidentiality. The incident described had to do with the analyst joining with his patient in a vigorous political discussion. Lander feels this is due to the analyst's making symmetry with the analysand, and so he highlights the ensuing need to develop an asymmetric analytic position. He seems to conflate confidentiality with anonymity. He comments on the fact that each time we are in symmetry, the analysis is in danger of suffering excessive distress that can push the analyst to break the promise of confidentiality (2003, 894).

I suspect that what Lander describes as symmetry, other analysts would call empathy; and what he alerts us to regarding the problem of staying in a symmetrical relationship, others would describe as the value of sustained empathy. Regardless of the use of words and without debating the value or danger of remaining in this analytic posture, the clinical vignette which Lander highlights as demonstrating "the incontinent analyst" is worthy of a critical examination.

If the analyst's overidentification with the patient results in a revelation of the analyst's own political feelings, it is arguable if that revelation constitutes a break in confidentiality rather than an expression of the analyst's humanity. It might also be argued whether Lander's position of "neither agreeing nor disagreeing" with the patient, all the while feeling quite strongly about the issue, is really in the patient's best interest. Some patients might feel that their analysts cannot help but have strong feelings and are merely suppressing them. This refusal to be open about such an issue will likely lead to a patient's fantasy about what the analyst might be thinking, and thus may uncover meaningful unconscious content. However, the refusal to be open may also lead to an entirely different set of fantasies if the patient recognizes that her silent analyst is neither agreeing nor disagreeing but merely not talking. There seems to be no good reason why an open political discussion could not itself be analyzed. There remains the possibility that the loneliness of the analytic position, along with what Landers terms some narcissistic deficiencies, at times may be responsible for the inability of the analyst to maintain confidentiality. For Landers, this is any expression of a value judgment as well as silence that is inappropriate to the occasion and is equally detrimental to the analytic process. This implication is offered as a given; that is, breaking confidentiality hurts the treatment. Once again Lander equates confidentiality, which usually involves a third party, with analytic disclosure per se.

Our two suggested categories of helping or hurting the treatment divide along the line of (1) a concentration on the effectiveness of the treatment, with particular concentration on transference-countertransference issues and (2) a separate focus on ethical issues involving a concern for the greater good. Thus, the reporting of a patient who was about to harm someone, as in the Tarasoff decision (Bollas and Sundelsen 1995, 4), is a clear "betrayal" of the patient in the interest of the protection of society. In contrast with this breach, one could readily see how writing up a patient for publication while getting the permission from the patient to do so (Dewald and Clark,

2001, 30) is a step aimed to both aid patients and benefit the greater good. However, the separation into the two categories may be a clue to one risk of confidentiality—a clue offered by the slight chink in the absolute armor of Bollas and Sundelsen: the consultation.

Case Illustration

Phil was a lawyer who, after a rather productive period in treatment which had resulted in a significant diminution of his presenting complaint of depression, came to somewhat of a standstill in his analytic work. Phil's analyst was troubled over the lack of progress in his otherwise valued patient, and he sought private consultation with a supervisor whom he had often gone to for assistance. Phil's analyst felt that he had much profited from this supervisory visit and returned to his patient with some new insights and vigor. Phil himself could not help but be aware of this change in his analyst's stance, and the analysis seemed now to proceed in a most promising direction. Shortly after this period of improvement, Phil asked his analyst why and how he accounted for this alteration in the treatment and even went so far as to inquire if the analyst had sought outside help. The analyst confessed—if that is the proper word—and Phil became outraged at what he felt was a breach of confidentiality. He had always felt this analysis to be a contract of privilege and privacy, but he had also thought of his analyst as possessed of all the knowledge necessary for his treatment. He was deeply disappointed.

Although this patient had in no way been identified to the supervisor and so clearly fell into the category of permissible breaches of confidentiality, it seems difficult to distinguish the issue from similar such actions, inasmuch as Phil had no concern as to his being identified. In this particular case there was a wonderful opportunity offered to analyze the patient's overidealization of his analyst and to work through the ensuing de-idealization. In retrospect Phil and his analyst saw this period of analysis as a moment of progress. Phil felt he could see the similarity in his rage at his father's shortcomings, and his analyst felt that he could better struggle with his own conflicts about needing help and having to do things on his own. This mutual benefit from the breach seemed to suggest more such benefits from some other breaches, with minor and major differences. This sort of consultation is the sole exception to confidentiality allowed, and it seems to hinge on helping the patient without revealing his identity. These two parameters seem worthwhile, but it remains to be seen if they can serve as guidelines to the entire problem surrounding confidentiality.

In this case they were of no use whatsoever and may even have created a difficulty.

The distinguishing point about this case has to do with the analyst's own psychology. Perhaps an analyst less able to struggle with his or her own inadequacies would not seek supervision, would pursue a different and less rewarding therapeutic action, or would even discontinue the analysis. If we focus on this single but crucial point, we may be able to construct a number of scenarios in which the analyst, constrained by confidentiality, would fail to do something which might benefit the treatment. Some of these scenarios could include identifying the patient as well. The inclusion of the third party does not come without a series of problems, risks, and even opportunities.

Case Illustration

Dr. G. analyzed a very volatile patient who had been placed on psychotropic medication by a consulting colleague of Dr. G's. The patient devoted many hours to lambasting the psychopharmacologist, whom the patient accused of being cold, insensitive, and downright sadistic. Some of this doctor's interventions seemed to be more harmful than helpful, and even undermining of the therapeutic work with Dr. G. Finally, Dr. G. called his colleague and asked about the interactions with the patient. Much to his surprise, he learned that this doctor had been a model of propriety and correctness, and many of the patient's vituperative attacks had been misplaced and distorted. Dr. G. compared this hostility toward his colleague with the overadoring attitude that the patient had toward him, and reluctantly became aware of the development and maintenance of a split transference involving these two therapists. Indeed, most of the negative feelings that may have been directed toward Dr. G. had been directed toward the psychopharmacologist. Dr. G. realized that he had enjoyed and participated in this arrangement, but he wondered if this problem would not potentially have existed in any analysis wherein one set of feelings were successfully diverted to a figure outside the analysis. However, something about this situation seemed different. There was a bona fide connection between these two doctors; Dr. G. had felt a need to be in touch with his patient's medication management, and he had made it a rule not to abdicate what he felt was a necessary responsibility. One of Dr. G's other colleagues divorced himself entirely from the pharmacological management of his patients, but Dr. G. felt that that position would make him more anxious and unable to intervene when necessary. Furthermore, he felt that his patient wanted him to be connected with the psychopharmacologist, and the conversation that resulted from his phone call was a necessary part of the treatment.

This case of a consultation with an identified patient opens the door a bit further than the single crack offered by Bollas and Sundelsen in the previous case, but the door should not be taken as a window of opportunity to dispense entirely with confidentiality. Rather, it might allow us to better understand the analyst's need to connect outside the consulting room, a need that is especially notable in cases of a split transference.

In an impressive essay Jonathan Lear states that analysis involves a transformation in which the analysand moves from "a condition to which he keeps secrets from himself to a condition in which he has a private life," and so psychoanalysis requires confidentiality as a means of modifying the results of repression. For Lear, "confidentiality is not just one value to be weighed against competing values; it is constitutive of the process itself" (2003, 5).

As telling as that position is, it is an example of a basic assumption that is usually valid but that merits scrutiny. Imagine a patient who, as a child, was involved in a secret sexual relationship with an adult and subsequently was unable to speak of it for fear of punishment of one sort of another. Often, these early instances of abuse are not repressed but disavowed (Goldberg 1999), and a treatment that was constituted around a premise and promise of secrecy could well be a reenactment of a traumatic childhood situation. We must be wary of any and all background assumptions, inasmuch as they may well inhibit our capacity to see. Of course, confidentiality is a central concept, but no concept should be taken for granted. We need recall that pragmatism insists that truth happens within the exigencies of a particular time and place.

Case Illustration

Mrs. S. had been a child of an early divorce followed by a quick remarriage of her mother to a man who sexually abused Mrs. S. Mrs. S. had endured this childhood trauma in complete silence, because she was convinced that reporting her stepfather's behavior to her mother would be overwhelming to this fragile woman, who had suffered enough from her first marriage. This vow of silence and secrecy followed her all through her adult life and was especially maintained in her weekly visits to her own father. That relationship was a loving and enjoyable one, but one equally marked by secrecy and concealment, inasmuch as Mrs. S.'s mother could not tolerate the idea that her daughter was happy with her ex-husband, the biological father of Mrs. S. Thus, the stage was set for Mrs. S. to live a life of compartments and concealments, a life which later manifested itself in addictive and delinquent behavior. By no means could one directly correlate such concealment and secrecy with the later delinquency, but it did seem to live on in much of this behavior.

Mrs. S. had treatment before coming to Dr. B., but she assumed from the start that he would never report anything about her to anyone; Dr. B. happily joined in this assumption. He soon learned, however, of both her repeated delinquency and misbehavior and the parallel concealment from her husband and her long list of therapists. She recreated her sad childhood configuration of not telling her mother about either father or stepfather, both of whom seemed to enlist her in somewhat pleasurable and forbidden behavior. This, not surprisingly, was also recreated in the transference, with the analyst either being unconsciously invited to collude in misbehavior (as described in a previous publication [Goldberg 1999]) or assigned the role of the knowing but mute parent.

As the patient's delinquency decreased in treatment and soon disappeared entirely, she became more and more depressed, and her legal problems now took center stage. She asked Dr. B. to write a letter to her lawyer, and he referred her to a legal consultant for this help, since he felt that this would breach confidentiality. It soon became clear to Dr. B. that only he could offer the necessary material for a legal defense, and he reluctantly did write a letter. Shortly after that, the patient's mother inexplicably asked the patient if her stepfather had ever abused her. The patient was flabbergasted at the truth finally coming out, and both she and Dr. B. wondered if some change had occurred within her that communicated itself to others: a change of bringing a split-off aspect of herself into an integrated whole. Of course, this seemed only a speculation that could not be verified, but it started the treatment on the road to integration.

No matter how anyone may evaluate this particular act of breaking confidentiality (that is, the letter to the lawyer), it would be problematic to classify it as derailing or damaging the analysis. Nor is it possible to say that it could have been completely avoided and still have the treatment continue. However, it may serve once again to blur the distinction between acts focused solely on helping the patient and those that go outside the treatment in both openly identifying the patient and enlisting others. The claim that one can rationalize many breaches of confidentiality by insisting that ultimately this is for the good of the patient, a claim disputed by Bollas and Sundelsen, is readily available in this and any case that allows the person to get the necessary treatment or to continue treatment. For Mrs. S.

the involvement of the lawyer allowed her to continue in treatment. We wonder further if the retreat to absolute confidentiality is but a place for the analyst to hide, especially from analyzing the precise nature of the third-party involvement.

Discussion

The exceptions to the physician-patient privilege that have developed over the years are considered by some so plentiful that the entire concept is without significance (Slovenko 1974). When one is invited to consider all the exceptions to both the privacy of the patient and the ethical requirements demanded of the clinician, there may be little room left for this "privilege," which is supposed to allow individuals to withhold information especially from the courts but also from a variety of interested parties. Without this privilege, enjoyed readily by priests, spouses, and lawyers, therapists are set adrift in a sea of ethical uncertainty. We quickly lose sight of our fundamental focus and become amateur ethicists and moralists.

To rescue ourselves from the life of bewilderment, we adopt rules of conduct such as in HIPAA which enable us to feel both honest and helpful, and surely one of the best of these rules is that of confidentiality. As the rule becomes confining and difficult to maintain, we begin to modify it. One modification is to obtain a patient's permission to break a confidence. Unfortunately, we have learned that patients are often unable to be free enough of transference issues to be in a position to really give informed consent. A patient may agree because of a positive feeling or disagree because of a negative one, while neither would accurately reflect an objective and rational decision. Another modification offered to aid our uncertainty is that of patient disguise, especially in terms of consultation or publication in professional journals. But this last is limited to patients who are not in the field and/or will not "come by such writing" (Bollas and Sundelsen 1995, 189). That, of course, excludes the possibility of writing about the valuable literature on the analyses of psychoanalytic candidates. At each and every turn we seem to confront a problem that seems more inhibiting either of our practice or of our freedom to function as members of a free society. If we limit ourselves to issues that deal only with the patient and the analyst, our first category, there probably can be no opening to a third party without a variety of implications: both good and bad. If we open the door to issues that go beyond the patient and the analyst, our second category, there can be no easy guideline to what is and is not allowable. I should like to propose a trial of a psychoanalytic solution to the quandary.

If we return to the fundamental thesis of the two books that compose the bulk of references in this chapter, it is that one must try to shut the door to any and all requests for information and intrusion by third parties. Ethical problems present themselves when the door is completely shut, but less so by far than when it is allowed to be ajar. Substituting "social therapists" as doorkeepers is one solution that effectively bypasses rather than solves the problem. The shut door is an absolute position that emphasizes the patient's welfare. The open door is a relative position that makes for the introduction of interests that may coincide with or override those of the patient. It may, however, also be helpful to make a psychoanalytic assessment of the inclusion of the third party without any preconceived value judgments.

The concept of a split transference, a vertical split as conceptualized in self psychology, directs our attention to a divided set of feelings: one group directed and focused on the analyst, another devoted to an area of concern and/or behavior in persons and issues outside the analysis. One obvious solution to this divide is to bring the split-off material into the analysis and onto the person of the analyst. This is not always an easy accomplishment, and sometimes an analyst may unwittingly keep the material out of the analysis. Consider as an aside a patient in analysis for approximately eight years who never mentioned to his analyst that he regularly stole books from his university bookstore. In a subsequent treatment he realized that this first analyst had communicated nonverbally to him that she could not handle that information. Thus, we see that it is up to the analyst to somehow allow the split-off material to participate in the analysis. This rather simple idea goes far beyond the analyst's willingness to listen to warded-off material, inasmuch as some of this material may present itself only in the form of behavior, as witnessed in the above-noted book thief, not ideation. There are patients who must be seen as unable to talk rather than as unwilling to do so. They are prone to inviting the analyst to collude with them rather than to interpret that about which they cannot speak.

If the analyst betrays the confidence of a patient by opening the door to a third party, he or she is essentially participating in an enactment but probably no more so than if the door is effectively barred. Both closing and opening are actions, but one is regularly more prized than the other. We are lulled into thinking that silence, like inactivity, is the proper atmosphere for analytic work, but there is no guarantee that free association prospers in a field of such deprivation. Surely, some patients may do well with a more responsive analyst, even though some analysts may feel most patients do best with the original parameters of conduct. Just as surely, there may be patients who do better with the action of an analyst who opens the door to consultants, psychopharmacologists, lawyers, and the like. The crucial issue is that of analyzing the action. I suspect this central element is ignored or neglected by the assumption of an absolutarian posture. If we are convinced that confidentiality is an absolute right, we become seduced into believing that it is beyond investigation and interpretation. It runs the risk of fading into the background and only being attended to in its breach. Unfortunately, too often such attention is composed of worry over ethical issues rather than of a careful examination of the transference implications of the presence of a third party. Of course, a relativist position invites other sorts of dilemmas.

The action of an analyst who breaks the bond of confidentiality is best thought of as one kind of enactment that demands investigation and interpretation rather than as an error of commission worthy of condemnation. This sort of stance treats analysis as an activity that corrects itself by the process of interpretation rather than one of adherence to a set of procedures and rules. Of course, we may not always be able to effectively understand and interpret our actions, but we are always better off wondering why we do what we do rather than chastising ourselves for supposed errors.

The entrance of a lawyer or an insurance company into the sanctity of the analytic dialogue, however welcome or unwelcome, turns the two-person dialogue into a conversation of three parties. Many times the analyst is blind to the transference implications of this entrance, but many other times the analysis will not or cannot proceed without such a connection. There need be no automatic injunction against the analyst examining privately or openly what this third person means to him as well as what that presence means to the patient. The exclusion of the lawyer or the insurance company may offer a feeling of comfort or smugness, but such exclusion could well assist in the analyst's remaining unaware of his or her unconscious motives in such rigorous rule adherence.

Summary

Absolute positions are snares that routinely betray their dangers by the introduction of selected exceptions. This is seen in the assumed and inviolate absolute basic right to confidentiality which begins with an exception allowed to consultation with a colleague and then proceeds to a list that seems to have no end. We soon seem to leave the arena of our expertise and move on to the domain of ethics. This is no brief against the proper concern with ethics but rather is an alerting call to our having missed the point. Once we become alert to standing in the wrong place, we tend to go back, to retreat to our absolutarian stance. Both directions, that of exceptions and that of retreat, make for a neglect of our work as analysts.

Embracing confidentiality as an absolute right runs a risk of allowing unconscious material which could be brought into the analysis to remain outside as split-off and unintegrated. In one sense, an analyst may collude with a patient in maintaining confidentiality as well as in breaching it. The former stance is supported by our established procedures and is typically and with good reasons embraced by our profession, but it is not one that should be immune from psychoanalytic inquiry. Opening the door to third parties is a move decried by our established procedures and is certainly a move to be very cautious in considering. However, it, too, should not be classified as a prohibition without exceptions. Both stances are too risky. Everything in analysis is to be seen as an interesting site for investigation and interpretation.

Conclusions

Psychoanalysis sits uneasily between an allegiance to a proper way to function and an openness to a variety of paths which can lead to a form of methodological anarchy. My personal solution to this delicate balance is to see analysis as an heir to the field of American pragmatism. What is demanded of us is an ever-ready alertness to whatever we may feel is taken for granted, all the while recognizing that we may need to abandon our yearning for something that we can all agree upon as grounding our inquiry (Goldberg 2002, 249). Just as absolute positions raise problems, so too do relative ones. As we have earlier said, pragmatism is not relativism, since at times the pragmatic path may espouse an absolute stand.

A reexamination of the promise of confidentiality as an absolute right of patients results in the same opening to uncertainty as happens in the reexamination of many of the seemingly unalterable rules and procedures of psychoanalysis. This sort of housecleaning can be upsetting to many of us who take comfort in the supposed proper conduct of an analysis under proper conditions. However, it is equally likely to cause a reconsideration of what many feel is the more correct and proper pursuit of psychoanalysis, that is, the understanding of a patient in depth. There may be no single road to achieve such a goal. However, such understanding may be made more difficult if we as therapists become armed with prejudices, which, unlike confidentiality, seem not to be rules but attitudes of propriety, as we shall see in the next chapter.

CHAPTER SIX

On the Nature of Thoughtlessness

Introduction

A good deal of moral weight lies behind the concept of thoughtfulness toward others, and so an equal balance of opprobrium is assigned to the counterpart of thoughtlessness. To tease these ideas apart from these moral standards and so to judge them from a psychological point of view might demand an objectivity that is usually beyond most of us. So it should be apparent that one easily, but perhaps wrongly, assigns thoughtfulness to maturity and health, while its absence becomes a sure sign of psychopathology. Perhaps one could introduce an inquiry into these opposite states or positions having this assigned value consideration in mind, and so could entertain the suggestion that even thoughtlessness can be seen as not so wholly awful. This is offered as an illustration of a moral stance that has possibly inhibited a form of inquiry because of covert assumptions about right and wrong and what makes for a good person. After all, keeping someone in mind with the added connotation of caring about that person is the recipe for thoughtfulness.

Case Illustrations

Meredith was married to a man who seemed to be possessed of all the desired virtues of a husband, but who was the target of much of Meredith's displeasure. She began one hour of therapy by telling her psychotherapist of a recent move of theirs to a new apartment. Don, her husband, had carefully arranged his computer and other varied electrical equipment according to his own needs and desires and when finished made this somewhat triumphant announcement to his wife, who then reminded him that her own computer with its accompanying equipment remained in its unusable state. Don was quite surprised, asked what he should do, and proceeded to attend to the task until fairly late into the night. Meredith reported these events to the therapist with the full recognition that none of this seemed so unusual; rather, she wished to underscore this particular trait of Don's— that is, he seemed both well-meaning and accommodating but rarely if ever aware of his wife's needs save after the fact. Once something was called to his attention, he usually readily complied, but often not without his being told just what he had to do. Don was both bright and eager to please, but rather at a loss as to just *how* to please. He seemed to perceive Meredith as someone to be pacified and mollified, and on those very rare occasions that he anticipated and fulfilled a job that was required, he would openly expect a hearty round of applause and appreciation. These events of thought-fulness were rare enough in their married life that they almost seemed to merit such an exaggerated response, but it was only reluctantly offered.

Meredith came from a family where she was clearly the star, and she soon exceeded her siblings in both education and achievement. Her marriage to Don was but another step on her ladder of success, but she somehow knew from the start that she was to be disappointed in her choice of husband. On the surface there was nothing to complain or worry about, but it soon became clear that Don saw Meredith as he did all women: as necessary but burdensome sources of worry and complaint. Once, when Meredith had injured herself at home and was lying on the bathroom floor, she managed to phone Don, who was about to tee off on the golf course. She explained her plight. He asked her what he should do. She was astounded. This episode seemed to serve as a template for her marital woes, and one that never seemed to be put to rest. If and when Meredith would point out this clear deficit to Don, he would feel guilty and try doubly hard to compensate in some manner or other. It soon became clear to them, and also not discussed further, that Don was quite unable to think about Meredith much, if at all. At least, in terms of Meredith, he was thoughtless. Whereas Don's thoughtlessness seemed focused primarily on women, it was by no means the case that women were its sole target. It extended to his parents and his children, who seemed resigned to and tolerant of it.

In vivid contrast with Don, Meredith was a strikingly thoughtful person who seemed to effortlessly engage in her many other-directed activities: calling friends, sending notes to the sick, bringing gifts for all occasions, and thinking of a multitude of other thoughtful and kind behaviors toward others. The feelings accompanying these actions were feelings that seemed denied to Don. He was able to conform to clearly communicated demands, but these conforming acts were primarily to avoid criticism and guilt. He never enjoyed his job of conforming. Meredith, on the other hand, experienced pleasure from being thoughtful; this pleasure needed no recognition or reward. She was genuinely thoughtful, while Don was just as genuinely thoughtless. She enjoyed thinking of others. He found it rather alien but unavoidable. There probably is little doubt that Meredith would be seen as both likeable and psychologically healthy, while Don would be tolerated and awarded one or another label of psychopathology.

What about Thought?

In order to determine if there is an explanation as to this sharp difference between Meredith and Don, it is necessary to gain some perspective as to when and why certain people are thoughtful and others thoughtless. Some insight may be gained from developmental considerations as well as from further clinical material. No attempt will be made here to review the enormous literature on the development of thought, but a brief guiding overview is in order. There has been a tendency in psychoanalysis to explain behavior on the basis of wayward infantile and childhood development in order to best reveal the crucial determinants of adult pathology. With today's move away from linear development, we recognize that there is no way either to make a claim for what constitutes normal development or to determine what gives rise to pathology.

Thinking is usually classified under cognition and so is separated from emotions. Whether or not this is a valid division, it is one that permits us an entrance into the field. Of course, the field is much too complex to be easily summarized, but for our purposes we can begin with the premises that thinking in humans demands some sort of language, verbal or otherwise, and that thought is always about something. Although one may argue that certain forms of abstract thinking as exemplified by mathematics or musical notations or computer programming are devoid of feeling, it seems unarguable that most thinking is inseparable from feeling. We here are considering thinking and caring about others.

Children are born into a sea of words, and language is felt to be programmed from birth. Traditional psychoanalysis posits that child development is also guided by programs that operate according to the pleasure principle. The thinking that unfolds in normal human development involves planning and reflecting, remembering and reminiscing, while its pathological components range from blocking to ruminating to all forms of obsessional thought. Since our minds are incapable of being without thought, we reserve the concepts of thoughtfulness and thoughtlessness for conscious activity, all the while recognizing that a failure to think of or about someone may be due to unconscious factors, just as a preoccupation with someone also may have an unconscious determinant.

If we put aside the occasional defects of thinking that arise from neurotic conflicts and manifest themselves in parapraxes such as forgetfulness, we can consider the widespread failure to be thoughtful, which seems to have a more characterologic flavor, that is, to be chronic and unrelenting. However, we can be easily tempted to conflate a failure to be thoughtful with a failure to be considerate, that is, thinking about another person. In fact, some people are quite thoughtful but not necessarily about others. To recall the philosopher Emmanuel Levinas, thoughtless people seem immune to a primordial relationship to the other. More about that will be discussed later, but it serves to remind us of the implicit assumptions about living the good and proper life.

Case Illustrations

Lester was a patient in analysis who periodically bored his analyst. One such occurrence consisted of a series of hours that seemed mainly to be reports of the day's events, until the moment when Lester's analyst sensed a feeling of excitement coming from his otherwise lackadaisical patient. The excitement had to do with Lester's reconfiguring his law office to make it completely paperless; every bit of information was to be electronically stored. As the patient continued to talk about his plans for his office, he managed to catch the interest of his analyst and so proceeded to share his enthusiasm for this electronic adventure of his with him. Lester's thoughts were consumed by the intricacies of the future electronic marvel he was constructing; one could hardly claim that this patient was not thoughtful. Rather, he had a different sort of thinking, one without other people but nonetheless filled with feeling and with meaning. As the analyst allowed himself to share this particular form of the patient's interests, he began to conceptualize this in theoretical terms. He felt that this new office of Lester's was an extension or a representation of the patient's self. His formulation of the psychological state of the patient was of a narcissistic preoccupation with an emerging grandiose fantasy which demanded a specific form of mirroring that, in turn, might well elicit a feeling of boredom from the listener. For this analyst, the patient's neglect of thoughts about their relationship simply reflected the diagnosis of a self-centered individual who was relatively incapable of investing much in others. Was this the underlying theme in all cases of thoughtlessness?

Compare Lester's intense preoccupation with wires and computer screens to Betsy's equally intense concerns regarding the impact of her efforts on others. Betsy was a charming and gregarious woman who spent a good deal of her day phoning or writing to friends and acquaintances, planning small get-togethers or large dinner parties, and worrying about what others thought of her. In contrast with Meredith, who seemed to enjoy writing a note or sending a gift for the sheer pleasure of contemplating the recipient's pleasure, Betsy seemed more pained until she found out just how much the recipient's appraisal of her had been altered or enhanced. That is to say that her thoughtfulness was clearly in the direction of a concern about herself rather that about another. To be sure, one may readily claim that Betsy was just as self-centered as Lester, and so the only thing that differentiated the two was Lester's focus on things that reflected back on him, while Betsy did the same with people. Otherwise they seemed to share a similar intensity of thought.

It should be clear that the overt behavior of any person in terms of thinking about or caring for another person is a very poor indicator of that person's ability or capacity to exercise what we might call thoughtfulness. Our four case vignettes range from Don, who seemed quite deficient in his grasp of the needs of others, to Meredith, who appeared to enjoy thinking and caring about others. Between these two we considered Lester, who, by the way, could regularly figure out what he might do for others but whose thought was primarily about things; and Betsy, who surely thought a lot about others but primarily as way stations to thinking about herself.

No doubt there are all sorts of gradations and mixtures of the qualities assigned to our four cases, but a useful continuum can be constructed in order to pursue our inquiry.

Sources of Thoughtlessness

It is not infrequently that a patient describes one or both parents as being either thoughtless or forgetful. From a Hollywood movie that depicts a family leaving a child behind when they set off on a vacation (*Home Alone*) to a forlorn tale of a child being abandoned in a store or on a beach or at a picnic, there does seem to be a bit of folklore that underscores the child who is simply not thought about and forgotten.

Not infrequently, a patient has fantasies about being the object of an analyst's thought. Some patients openly wonder if the analyst has thought about, worried about, or perhaps even missed them over the weekend or during a vacation. Whereas many analysts tend to inquire about and determine if and how the patient missed or thought about *them* during an absence, the obverse seems to carry an equal weight. In fact, many queries of analysts about their significance are scoffed at because they may run in the wrong direction and rarely become modified.

Case Illustration

Not too long after Gregory had been in analysis, it became clear that his father was and had been a rather peculiar person. Material gathered from the transference along with the historical descriptions of the father seemed to suggest that he suffered from some variant of Asperger's syndrome. Gregory's father was an actuary at a national insurance company, and although he had never achieved noteworthy financial success, he had managed to acquire an important position along with the reputation of being a reliable employee. Gregory would describe the family's being taken to a museum by his father, who would spend hours reading all of the descriptions of all of the displayed objects and mementos. Gregory's father would become fairly oblivious of what the rest of the family had to endure, although it was clear that he meant them no discomfort. His obliviousness of his family's presence extended to the home, where he would walk around in various states of undress, forget the names of his children at regular intervals, eat his meals in a direction of unusual sequences often beginning with dessert, and on and on.

The impact on Gregory of this bizarre and thoughtless person cannot, of course, be readily calibrated because of the availability of Gregory's mother, who was described as someone who happily tolerated her somewhat strange husband and rarely called attention to his aberrant behavior.

One quality that seemed to result from being raised by this set of parents was of Gregory's being very anxious not to intrude upon or take up residence in his analyst's mind or indeed in any other person's mind. Subsequent analytic work only minimally confirmed the defensive nature of this apprehension, since Gregory felt that there was no room for him in his parents' (and now analyst's) thoughts. Gregory, on the other hand, seemed similar to the earlier case of Meredith in that he was endlessly thoughtful of and concerned about others. He also showed genuine pleasure at the idea of doing something for someone else.

The clinical evidence from many practitioners would suggest that thoughtful parents do *not* necessarily lead to thoughtful children, nor do thoughtless parents spawn a generation of like-minded offspring. This lack of a one-to-one correlation results both from the complexity of the concept and from the multiplicity of contributing factors. One is probably on solid ground in claiming that narcissistic preoccupation can give the impression of thoughtlessness and that the wish to be thought of is fairly ubiquitous and unrelenting.

Thinking of Others

Although psychoanalysis subscribes to the concept of empathy as a data-gathering operation in which the observer is described as either identifying with the observed or putting oneself in the other's shoes, it is assumed that such information collection does not in itself necessarily have a moral or ethical dimension. We can be empathic with a person to whom we wish to sell a used car, while a surgeon may be unempathic with a person whose breast cancer he is removing. Doing good and being thoughtful need not be comrades in arms. Once we put to the side the associated positive valence to thoughtfulness, a better understanding of its psychological significance may emerge.

From a psychoanalytic viewpoint the study of conscious phenomena is a limited one. Unless one can unearth the unconscious motivations behind these conscious derivatives, there always exists a question as to the full meaning of the phenomena. If, for instance, one does not think of someone or something, this absence can be due to repression as well as to lack of concern. So, too, the thought of someone may serve as a displacement from another source. There is no doubt that a fuller explanation of thoughtfulness and thoughtlessness requires an in-depth inquiry, but it is difficult to make the claim that defensive maneuvers such as repression and displacement are close to a full explanation. The crucible of the transference does seem to confirm that some patients rarely think of others, some think primarily of the nonhuman, some think of others only to the extent that it enhances themselves, some worry endlessly about being thought about by others, and some seem truly thoughtful of others.

To return to Gregory, who had a parent who appeared to be psychologically unable to keep others in mind, some interesting issues did arise in the transference. Although Gregory himself was thoughtful and seemed to expect little in return, a remarkable and significant change seemed to occur when he began to feel recognized and thought about. We often postulate the need of the child to feel kept in mind by the mother, and Margaret Mahler's (1975) work of separation-individuation highlights a developmental step for a child who feels so remembered.[1] Being remembered when out of sight is certainly a different experience from being mirrored (Kohut 1971), inasmuch as the latter seems to demand an immediacy of experience, while the former contains continuity and stability. With Gregory's development of a conviction that he had a place in his analyst's mind, there came an alteration in Gregory's experience of his physical body. Initially, Gregory was anxious about wanting and needing to be remembered, but gradually he gained a new sense of solidity and a new way of thinking about himself. This is more properly considered as self constancy and so differs from object constancy.

As Gregory felt more and more connected to his analyst, the pleasure that ensued from this sense of belonging soon became mixed with or contaminated by a feeling of obligation and responsibility. There was no doubt about a countertransference experience of his analyst, who wanted to be thought of and about in his absence. On rethinking these events, the analyst felt that this was not so much countertransference as it was an expected and expectable reciprocity of thoughtfulness. Alas, Gregory wanted to be purely thought about without a corresponding obligation; it hardly seemed to be possible. Thoughtfulness became a burden and thoughtlessness a relief.

The empathic stance of the analyst who gathers psychological data from the patients is always matched by a similar, albeit different, effort on the part of patients. Patients read analysts just as they themselves are read, and so the reciprocity of psychologic interest operates with all the associated benefits and burdens of mutual understanding. There may be a moment in development wherein one feels some form of unadorned thoughtfulness, but it probably is short-lived.

Gregory's changed attitude about his body, his appearance, and his health moved on to a changed sense of how he looked to others. I cannot say if there was a corresponding alteration in his consideration of others, inasmuch as Gregory had always been rather thoughtful. However, this shift does seem to suggest that certain alterations in narcissistic deployment follow that of investment in objects. In this patient, as in so many others, the concern about the appraisal of others was always tinged with feelings of shame or guilt, and this was clearly connected to a childhood spent with a preoccupied parent. So for starters we can say that development requires

---

1. It may seem relevant at this point to discuss Winnicott and the alien self and Fonagy (2001) on mentalization, but such a discussion seems too far afield and complex for the main thesis.

a sense of being thought about, and this invokes a feeling of obligation to do the same for the other. Yet defects in this experience need not lead to a failing in being thoughtful of others. This would seem to buttress the notion of separate lines of development.

Once we concentrate on the narcissistic line of development, we see that it can take the form of concern about things or about people in which the goal is that of self-enhancement. This concern is not easily distinguished from the thoughtfulness we prefer to consider as genuine. In the strict sense of the term, the former type of concern surely qualifies as thoughtful.

If we follow the developmental line of objects, we see it has its own complexity. Sometimes it seems pure and pleasurable, but at other times it becomes weighted down with guilt and obligation. Meredith seemed to be thoughtful without a price. Gregory seemed to evidence both experiences. Perhaps Meredith's husband, Don, sought refuge in his own selfish pursuits to escape the issues of guilt that for him always accompanied thinking of others. One might even question Meredith's choice of a mate who was so opposite in nature.

A Philosophical Aside

Once one begins even a cursory investigation of religious and philosophical interest in the topic of concern about and thinking about others, there is an immediate awareness of an implicit rule of responsibility. Martin Buber and Emmanuel Levinas are perhaps the best contemporary exponents of the insistence that such responsibility is not a psychological relation or a product of conscious thought (Hand 1996, 66), but "ontological," or having to do with one's very existence. Buber says, "Man can become whole not by virtue of a relation to himself but only by virtue of a relation to another self" (ibid.). This certainly seems true in what we feel is the necessary state of the child's feeling that she has a place in her parents' mind. However, this is said primarily from a psychological perspective. Levinas extends the idea of responsibility for the other to the point of being responsible for whatever the other is responsible for. He says that one must and should put oneself in the place of the other, even to the point of death. One may agree with Levinas or attribute his position to a profound psychological naïveté. The latter stance recognizes that people develop along different trajectories, and so we cannot and should not moralize about differences that lead to determinations that are not under personal and conscious control. No matter whether one considers religion or psychology primary or foundational, it does seem to be the case that certain aspects of theological thinking are at odds with what we know to be "true" from our own understanding of depth psychology. This conflict may well be due to an inability to separate these ways of thinking or else may be due to a failure to reach a happy integration. The first failure is seen in our embrace of a moral dimension in assessing our patients and thereby assigning thoughtlessness to pathology. The second, the lack of integration, results from scholars like Levinas dismissing psychoanalysis without knowing what exactly they are dismissing. Both psychology and philosophy suffer from this insularity and troublesome interaction.

Discussion

Everyone has an opinion about thoughtlessness, and these opinions tend to close the door on efforts to understand and explain it. Explanations range from a conviction that biologically, women are naturally more thoughtful than men; that one can inculcate thoughtfulness along with charitable giving in children by example; that it is a fundamental grounding of religion, as exemplified in the Golden Rule; and so on. Thoughtlessness is not the same as being without thought, but rather is an indictment of selfishness and, in psychoanalytic terminology, of pathological narcissism, which can sometimes be treated and successfully result in care and consideration of others. To be sure, so-called thoughtless people may be thinking a great deal, but these thoughts are those that lead inevitably to self-enhancement and should be disposed of and dismissed.

When we evaluate the existence and degree of thoughtlessness in patients, we find a range of complexity that defies the usual opinions. Some supposedly thoughtless persons are able to think a lot about others and so are seen as thoughtful; however, they are serving their personal self-esteem and so end up as thoughtless. Some think a great deal about things rather than persons but still manage to be thoughtful of others. Some few seem almost incapable of the mindfulness of another person, and no amount of treatment seems to change them. None of this variety deserves condemnation.

When we evaluate the degree and existence of thoughtfulness in patients, we find an equal range of complexity. Some, as noted above, appear thoughtful but only in a selfish effort, while some descriptively selfish people can be quite caring of others. Some few persons seem to be genuinely thoughtful and derive a great deal of pleasure from acts of generosity, while others feel a guilt that can only be relieved by such acts. And so such acts may well not be deserving of applause.

Mindfulness does seem to be an essential ingredient in early development when parent and child find themselves in each other. However, this developmental achievement does not necessarily lay the groundwork for future caring for others. Although this may be a controversial conclusion, it merits further study. The sense of solidity and presence for the self seems to allow future development along either narcissistic or object-relational lines.

Summary and Conclusions

Psychoanalysts like to think that the subjectivity that enters into their practice can be studied and scrutinized and so reduced to a minimum. It seems not surprising that a good deal of this subjectivity is allowed to go unexamined and unrecognized on the basis of what is considered unquestioned and unquestionable. Much of this "taken for granted" material falls under moral and ethical guidelines, and thoughtfulness and thoughtlessness are readily seen as belonging to such material.

At a minimum, a careful unpacking of otherwise unassailable issues ranging from confidentiality to responsibility to all sorts of rules of conduct can only be of benefit to the psychoanalyst's wish for objectivity. One such examination of the issue of thinking of others is shown to be interwoven with moral points of view. The scrutiny of these concepts allows for an appreciation of their complexity and a differentiation from what is often felt as self-evident. This exercise is offered as an opening to future examination of the background assumptions of psychoanalysis. Next we shall see how moral assumptions can interfere with the conduct of treatment.

CHAPTER SEVEN

I Wish the Hour Were Over: Elements of a Moral Dilemma

Introduction

A patient in psychoanalysis, shortly after contemplating and then voicing agreement with an interpretation that had been offered, announced an intense urge to get up and leave—that is, wishing the not-yet-terminated analytic hour were at an end. Yet no sooner had this thought been uttered than there followed another wish of possibly equal intensity: that the hour not soon end. One might readily say that this patient was ambivalent about staying versus leaving, and surely it could also be said that he was in conflict about these two impulses or feelings.

The interpretation that had just been offered had to do with a somewhat corresponding set of issues in conflict, these having to do with the patient's father. Although initially this patient voiced only negative and disdainful memories and feelings about his father, over time he had recalled more and more positive emotions about this parent, and eventually he had been able to contemplate how much the loss of his father meant to him. This trauma had occurred when the patient was ten years old, resulting from an acrimonious separation and divorce. Although this had first been presented by the patient as an episode of relief to all (the patient, his mother, his older sister, and his younger brother), it now served as the carrier of memories of both sadness and longing for the absent man.

The aforementioned relief of the household over the father's departure had been accompanied by an assignment to the patient of the role of man of the house—an assignment made by his mother, and one he had fulfilled with much satisfaction and pride. And so the conflict about departing the analytic hour early seemed to serve as a miniature enactment of that childhood event in that getting up to leave allowed him to feel independent and no longer in need of his analyst, while remaining a patient for the rest of the hour became associated with the never-relieved sadness and yearning of the forlorn little boy. We seemed to be present at a paradigmatic illustration of conflict.

Multiple Perspectives on Ambivalence and Conflict

In "Inhibitions, Symptoms, and Anxiety," Freud presents his prototypical version of a conflict due to ambivalence, positing the case of Little Hans as demonstrating a "well-grounded love along with a no less justifiable hatred" ([1926] 1953–74, 21:102). Freud states that although this conflict may well lead to a symptom such as the phobia in Little Hans, it may also be resolved by way of an intensification of one of the two feelings and the vanishing of the other. Although the conflict arises from ambivalence, there may be no evident trace of either of the forces of opposition. The two feelings are no longer experienced consciously, and the conflict has now moved to another arena.

That move and disappearance of conscious conflict has been described in modern psychoanalysis as one existing between posited agencies of the mind. Thus, as the loving feelings of the little boy toward the father remain conscious, the hostile ones are kept at bay by the strength and opposition of the superego. Of course, the loving ones may be repressed and vanish as well.

The simple formula of ambivalence is now a complicated complex, with some ambivalence being conscious and remaining so; some leading to conflict that in turn may give rise to a symptom such as a phobia, or to a reaction formation in which overwhelming love drives away the hostility, or vice versa; and some simply seeming to vanish altogether. Indeed, the universality of both ambivalence and conflict gives one license almost to dispense with the specific meanings of the words. We can be ambivalent about the choice of a dessert, in conflict about a particular career decision, and seemingly free of either issue while the struggle remains an unconscious one.

It may be prudent to recognize that much ambivalence lies outside the usual meaning of conflict, as when one goes back and forth in choosing a particular piece of clothing for an ensemble, while some conflict may seem to be without ambivalence, as when we rid ourselves of an annoying fly or mosquito. The significance of Freud's presentation was to underscore the presence of opposition in the form of love versus hate. And the further import of his illustration was to position this opposition within the psyche, thus identifying it as an internal and constant struggle.

Keeping these simple perspectives in mind—internal, oppositional, and unconscious—I would like to offer a puzzle: a form of conflict that appears at times to satisfy none of these requirements, yet paradoxically also qualifies as conflict. This form of conflict is represented by the narcissistic behavior disorders, which range from cross-dressing to thievery to all manner of substance abuse. They are external for all to see. They exist sometimes though not always without a sense of opposition, and they are conscious without exception. For sure, one sees a variety of qualifications to these points, but for the most part they are conflicts that seem to defy the neatness of an internal, unconscious opposition of mental agencies. Many of these patients are completely aware of what they do and are not at all in conflict about it while they are doing it. Yet they unhesitatingly insist that they dislike or even despise these behaviors in retrospect, presenting them on those occasions as a conflict. They are miniaturizations of Jekyll and Hyde, and, as Robert Louis Stevenson wrote: "Henry Jekyll stood *at times* aghast at the acts of Edward Hyde" ([1886] 2003, 67; emphasis in the original). And we all recall that this divide was between good and evil.

Some Theoretical Ways of Conceptualizing Behavior Disorders

The theoretical underpinnings of narcissistic behavior disorders have been presented in detail elsewhere (Goldberg 1999) with reference to a variety of clinical case studies (Goldberg 2001). The crucial distinction offered to explain this form of disorder is that of a focus on the mechanism of disavowal utilizing the concept of the vertical split. This configuration presents a psyche that is divided into two usually unequal, parallel sectors. These sectors are separated from each another and are initially characterized by having different and often opposing sets of goals and values. Thus, a seemingly proper and mature heterosexual man might coexist with one having a periodically active involvement in some sexual perversion. The activation of the perverse sector, of whatever form it takes, is episodic, yet that sector is capable of a complete domination of this man's personality. After the perverse activity subsides, there may be remorse and regret, and so these parallel sectors qualify as being in conflict and oppositional, yet the one or the other regularly submits to the control of its counterpart and the opposition disappears.

What has become apparent in further studies of such behavior disorders is the lack of their confinement to the usual outstanding and dramatic forms of misbehaviors, such as the sexual perversions, and the recognition of similar configurations present in more subtle and common examples of conflict. Due either to our alertness to the existence of the phenomenon or to our reorientation in the ways of conceptualizing clinical material, we can now recognize the operation of disavowal and the existence of the vertical split in the wider variety of maladies. Thus, we can revisit an analytic patient and his or her presumed conscious conflict with an eye to ascertaining the likelihood of the patient's possession of parallel selves in a struggle (a conflict) to dominate and gain control of the psyche and the motoric mechanisms of behavior.

The Moral Conflict

To return to the patient of mine whom I described earlier, the initial examination of his battle between leaving and staying in the analytic hour, between independence and dependence, turned out rather surprisingly to me to be a moral conflict as well. We should all be familiar with what may be considered everyday and common (to therapists at least) moral conflicts. These range from our billing insurance companies for missed appointments, to changing diagnostic codes in order to ensure the payment of claims, to not declaring cash payments as income subject to income tax, to employing family members in mock positions in order to claim deductions, to moonlighting on top of salaried jobs that forbid outside employment, to claiming deductions that are personal forms of dining and entertainment as business-related, and on and on. It is a rare professional who has not at one time or another been forced to consider and even to struggle with one or another of these issues, and it is probably an equally rare one who has not in some manner rationalized the embrace of one or more items on this very abbreviated list. The active involvement in such an activity that might be considered immoral or illegal is felt by some to be a game of getting away with as much as possible and by others as an indicator of not conforming to a strict code of propriety. Regardless of where one stands, the differentiation between saints and sinners is not an easy one.

Clinical Case Elaboration

In order to maintain confidentiality, I shall offer only that a particular psychoanalytic patient of mine, the one referred to above, was an active participant in one of these immoral ventures, and this fact became clear at the very start of the analysis. When I first learned of it, I had not a whit of personal condemnation, feeling it to be both *justified*—in that it was a perfectly proper thing to do, and *justifiable*—in that I and my patient could readily explain and support this sort of behavior. Thus, the supposed moral dilemma was initially without a voice.

My patient's peccadillo was not unfamiliar to me, and it seemed further legitimized by his having been given a form of a "don't ask, don't tell" injunction by a superior when he first inquired about it. Thus, the two of us conspired in an agreement that seemed to highlight the peculiar bind that is practiced and indeed forced upon so many people who continue to live by necessity in areas of moral and ethical discomfort. Of course, I do not offer this as anything more than a further bit of armor in the defense of one's ultimately unacceptable behavior.

Indeed, this behavior *did* become openly unacceptable when the patient announced one day that a particularly stupid act of his had led to the exposure of his heretofore secret misdeeds. As he described to me the foolish bit of behavior that led to his exposure, and as he asked me if it were possible that he himself had unwittingly and unconsciously brought about his own state of shame and embarrassment at being "caught in the act," I was unable to do much more than offer the opinion that I felt it unlikely that he wanted to get caught. Thus, we became further joined, now in stupidity.

Much of this patient's treatment after the disclosure of his misdeed seemed focused on my championing his efforts to feel righteous and vindicated in what he had done, and there can be no doubt that I was quite unable to reach some midpoint of neutrality, or at least of analytic detachment, for quite some time. I cannot now be certain as to the moment at which I finally managed that feat, but it was certainly after our analytic work revealed the father as a man who was himself wrapped in corruption and double-dealing, primarily with members of his own family. I am convinced that my own recognition of a personal and private moral dilemma did not arrive as a bolt from the blue, but instead grew out of a succession of uncomfortable feelings that were triggered by my efforts to see the situation from the point of view of my patient's protagonist. I think it is vitally important that one live for a while in this gray area of conflict. Although any psychoanalyst must or should have at least a touch of larcenous leanings in order to really help a thief, it is an equal requirement that a period of uncertainty be allowed to have its day.

I vividly recall presenting some of these ideas to a group of psychoanalysts in Philadelphia, when one analyst responded by recounting a vignette of a patient who had stolen a dress from a department store, and who then asked her analyst what he thought of her. He proudly told the audience that he had informed his patient she was a thief, after which he triumphantly sat down. My private thought was that she of course knew that she was a thief and hardly needed him to tell her that. What she needed, and what he could not supply, was for him to experience her conflict. Living in uncertainty is not as easy as it sounds, since we know that most of our patients with behavior disorders do instead live in alternating periods of certainty. Surviving in the limbo of a dilemma is necessarily uncomfortable, and one is tempted to come down vigorously with a definitive pronouncement, just as did that unhelpful man in Philadelphia. However, the capacity to sustain the parallel state of supposed opposition is the first step in the achievement of a hoped-for integration of what has previously been split apart.

Integration does not by any means gain victory by favoring good over evil. Just as we all know or should know that forensic psychiatry has no room to breathe, what with the prevalent McNaughton rule of only knowing and acting upon right from wrong, we should also know that mere cognitive certainty is a poor guide to emotional conviction. It is especially difficult in our efforts to comprehend misbehavior for us to realize that what seems to be wrong beyond a shadow of a doubt is not simply to be judged according to the dimensions of right and wrong. Indeed, I finally succeeded in seeing that what my particular patient had done could have relatively equal support on both sides of the question. And so I was left with the proper stance for any analyst: a state of puzzlement, a condition that must necessarily precede that of understanding and eventual resolution.

Analysts are not good moral barometers, despite their wish to be so. Our primary tool of interpretation represents but one way of looking at things amid a myriad of such ways. When we offer an interpretation, it is an invitation to the patient to appreciate a new and different perspective, but it cannot completely erase the point of view that the patient has lived by up until now. As much as we might like to feel that we know best, it is better to know that we only know differently.

The difficult task of integrating disparate points of view is no more one of reaching a compromise than it is of choosing one over the other. It is here that psychoanalysis offers a unique perspective by its claim of being a depth psychology: we must attend to what lies beneath this duality of purpose, a hint of which was offered to me by my patient in his announced struggle to leave or to stay.

A Dual Transference

The vision of the father retained by this patient was realized by his seeing me as a bright and competent figure on one hand, and as a corrupt and somewhat doddering fool on the other. Statements that I had made in one hour came back as deliveries by the patient in a much transmogrified form several days later, sounding like the mutterings of an idiot. My much sought-after and happy neutrality was continually on the edge of being destroyed by a vigorous defense of mine—one aimed at clarification and a restoration of me as possessing unappreciated wisdom. Yet at times I was convinced that I was indeed a fool, and so I made a silent resolve to keep my mouth shut. (Perhaps some of the long silences commonly attributed to analysts derive from a similar sort of resolution.)

My patient seemed different from Little Hans, not so much in his possession of "well-grounded love along with a no less justifiable hatred" (S. Freud [1926] 1953–74, 21:102)—both of which were quite apparent—as in his failure to reconcile these emotions by way of identification with both aspects of his father. It became clear to me that he had suffered a traumatic de-idealizaton of a father who, in one sense, remained always outside of him and for whom he had conducted a relentless search. And what lay beneath this oscillation between the great and the belittled, the good and the bad, and all the other possible dualities was the depression that wrapped itself around him when he admitted to wanting to stay in the hour. The very recognition and articulation of that wish introduced him once again to an empty sadness that he now recalled had enveloped him when his father left home. He could try with limited success and urging from his mother to replace his father, thereby covering this inner feeling of emptiness—or he could vent his rage at the departed and disappointing father in a different but equally unsuccessful effort to obliterate his depression. Interestingly enough, one psychiatrist had earlier diagnosed him as having bipolar disorder.

The patient's split of the representative hour and those that followed could be said to mesh nicely with that of the analyst in his parallel, complementary split. We both knew right from wrong, yet had chosen a course based on a set of rationalizations that drowned out the legal issues. While never blind to the sector that we had chosen to disavow, we gave it little heed until it slowly began to make a claim to recognition. At some undetermined point, we became locked in a moral dilemma and remained there until further psychoanalytic work revealed some of its origins.

I have here presented my main points about this analysis by focusing on the father, with little reference to the patient's mother. I do so in the interest of brevity, as well as out of my wish to pursue the line of inquiry introduced by Freud in regard to Little Hans. Surely, no study of depression can be considered complete without an examination of the early maternal relationship. Nevertheless, this patient's life story did seem to founder on the rocks of some core depression that had telescoped into the time of the loss of his father, and it was there that the work of analysis came to be concentrated. And so it is there that one answer to the connection between psychoanalysis and morality can be focused. This is not to say that all moral conundrums are fundamentally psychological problems, but it is to suggest that psychoanalysis may have a contribution to make to issues of morality. Moral principles are not to be seen strictly as either exclusively God-given or intrinsic to humanity, but as solutions to psychic discontent as well.

The Contribution of Disavowal to Superego Explanations

The classical explanations for moral lapses have to do with the power and position of the superego as presented in the tripartite model of the mind. Failures in the strength and integrity of the superego allow for the escape of immoral or amoral action. Sometimes this has been conceptualized in the form of superego lacunae (Gedo and Goldberg 1973, 14) and at other times as an identification with a criminal sort of superego (Benedek 1973, 246). The feeling that dominates this oppositional scene is that of guilt, and the predominant defense that is operable or absent is that of repression.

A different model of the mind was first presented by Freud (1927) in his discussion of fetishism, where the predominant defense was that of disavowal. This was further elaborated by Kohut as a disorder of narcissism, illustrated by the positing of separate self configurations split off from each other. Neither model can or should claim exclusivity, since models ought to be viewed as conveniences or tools of explanation rather than as factual representations.

Disavowal, again according to Freud, has to do with perception of the reality of castration: either one has a penis or one does not. In its more familiar usage as denial, once again we see it in the denial of bereavement over a lost one, as well as in all sorts of common ways that the real world is not allowed to exist. When we move to moral issues, it becomes a case of the forbidden being allowed, owing to the absence of that reality. From the commandments of religion to the injunctions of law, one is confronted with choices and options, to do or not to do, and the denial of the one allows the other. All the "thou shalt nots" become abandoned or erased by the process of denial, following the law of two negatives that yield a positive. All the boundaries vanish through the employment of disavowal.

If we return to the more obvious standards of the allowable, the study of behavior disorders enables us to better study the vertical split in individuals who are grossly aberrant. We are now able to see this split as operant in much more subtle kinds of struggles over what is proper and what is improper. And the inevitable conclusion is that there is no clear and unmistakable point at which a moral conflict moves from the minor to the significant, and so any and all such differences become a proper arena for psychological study.

The model of the superego in conflict with forbidden impulses arises in psychoanalysis by a transference displacement from patient to analyst—that is, the analyst becomes the bearer of superego prohibitions, and the struggle takes place between analyst and patient. Thus, Little Hans might see his analyst as the embodiment of the superego, as one who would condemn and punish him for erotic feelings toward his mother and hostile ones toward his father. Agencies of the mind are expressed in transference interactions. However, conflicts in these forms of narcissistic disorders often take a different form—they become realized within the person of the analyst, who matches the patient's personal split. Thus, the patient's misdeed is not enacted and condemned in the interaction between patient and analyst, but rather it is recognized as a conflict that is then experienced by the analyst. I do not tell my patient that he is wrong, so that together we can analyze the origins of his struggle with its possible ensuing guilt. I feel that his misdeed is justified at the same time that I feel it is wrong, and so I share his split. Unless I can do so, I may as well sit in mutual triumph with my colleague in Philadelphia as a bearer of correctness.

Discussion

Pluralism seems to predominate in today's psychoanalysis, but it runs the risk of engendering a certain laxity in the clarity and coherence of our thinking—while it also provides an opportunity to try out various perspectives in the effort to explain mental operations. It is certainly no radical move for us to consider a more central role for disavowal, and it is reasonable to suggest that the transference configurations relevant to disavowal will have a corresponding distinction from those witnessed in the mental model underscoring repression. Disavowal invites a scrutiny of reality. The objective analyst aims at realistic appraisal of the position or perception offered by a patient, and may respond accordingly; for example, "You are wrong in seeing the world that way." We see this in the work of mourning, wherein the patient has to accept the fact of his or her loss. The empathic analyst is able to be realistic, but needs to share the disavowed sector as well; for example, "You are correct to want the world to be different." My point is that the analyst, like the patient, can be both objective and empathic, thereby living simultaneously in what are essentially two visions of the world—visions in conflict.

One other unremarkable but often forgotten contribution to the conviction that one is correct and one is doing right is a feeling of pride and righteousness. The corresponding or complementary feeling attributable to uncertainty and error is often depression. This can be related, of course, to the vicissitudes of the operations of the superego, but, as in my patient described earlier, it can also represent the underlying depression found in many instances of disavowal. I suspect that further study of the types of transferences that present themselves in more subtle forms of behavior in conflict will lead to a deeper understanding of the qualities and treatment of various forms of depression.

Summary and Conclusions

The preeminent position of intrapsychic conflict in some psychoanalytic circles merits rethinking, with an eye to seeing it as but one way of examining and explaining a variety of oppositional struggles, ranging from indecision to ambivalence to reaction formation to all manner of symptomatology. The battle between instinctual drives and their control is an oversimplified truism that has failed to fully explicate the complex and different forms of transferences that emerge in psychoanalytic encounters.

The best available evidence for confirmation of a different way to think about a wide range of oppositional phenomena is gained by examining different forms of transference manifestations. Viewing disavowal as not only a defense offers us an opportunity to expand our theoretical vision. The particular form of transference seen in those who employ disavowal is a correlation of the vertical split in the patient to one that develops and emerges in the therapist or analyst. The split-apart sectors are often seen in opposition to each other, with one corresponding to reality (the reality ego) and one demonstrating a disregard of reality (the "misbehaving" sector). Psychoanalytic phenomena encourage a matched split in the analyst, reflective of the psychic makeup of the patient.

Analytic work involves the integration of these divided sectors, with particular attention to the underlying depression that seems to regularly characterize these patients. Interpretations of the drive-defense model may be more disabling than helpful, while interpretations of the dual sectors are experienced as ameliorative. As always, the best principle to follow in psychoanalysis is that of the interpretation of the transference, with the added recognition that transference takes many different forms. We shall examine this in more detail in chapter 11, on deontology. We next turn to a different sort of moral dilemma that has legal overtones.

CHAPTER EIGHT

Psychotherapy and Psychoanalysis and the Problem of Ownership: An Effort at Resolution

Ownership implies property, something that one has or holds. For the most part the concept of ownership would more properly be examined as an issue involving legal considerations and hardly at all as one belonging to the province of psychology or psychoanalysis. Yet the powerful feeling of having something, or indeed someone, belong to you and the equally potent feeling that comes from belonging to another individual or group make the idea of ownership amenable to the tools and theories of a discipline devoted primarily to the mind.

The relevance of such a study would reside in the arena of a better understanding of the meaning of ownership. This understanding could aid us in unraveling the conundrum that plagues students of psychotherapy and psychoanalysis: how best to delineate the intrapsychic, the interpersonal, and the newly popular intersubjective. The hope for an agreed-upon resolution of just where fantasies, thoughts, and conflicts reside is a hope without fulfillment as long as one is committed to what at best is a geographic solution. The prefixes *intra* and *inter* presume the issue of placement. By refocusing the problem to an area of study that avoids concern about placement, we may be able to answer the otherwise unanswerable and so effect a resolution of sorts.

In a similar vein, questions about the mind and the brain might also yield some new solutions. While no one doubts that the brain resides within the skull and that this brain surely gives rise to the mind, there are legions of doubters as to whether the mind is the brain or possibly lives elsewhere. Our language may have led us into corridors without an escape, and so a change in the conversation may point to an exit. The problem to be addressed is primarily one of language but one that is not peculiar to psychoanalysis. It will be presented here as a problem that crosses many disciplines.

It may also be seen as a moral issue, since property rights inevitably lead to questions of right and wrong. We see it in arguments over who is the rightful heir to contested wills, who is the rightful owner of frozen embryos, who is the real mother in adoption suits, and on and on. It also becomes an issue that is not often recognized in psychoanalysis and psychotherapy.

Realism

What may seem at first to be a wide detour around the present question may in fact aid in finding a solution. The detour begins with the recognition that psychoanalysts from Freud to the present live with the legacy of naïve realism. That is to say that the average analyst believes that there is a real world out there which is correctly sensed by our organs of perception and thereby is a world that is shared by those of us with similar such organs. When we look at an apple, we see an apple that we can study as that apple out there. The same follows for each and every component of the external world. We are convinced that we are a camera that has an internal viewer to check for accuracy and to adjust for more careful calibration. The same therefore applies to the book you are now reading, as well as the hands that hold that book. The world is all out there and is much the same for all of us.

In truth, all that occurs which allows us to feel that we know the world out there is a complex series of electrochemical reactions going on in the brain. There is no camera, no little apple or book in the head, and no little person sitting in a theater looking at that apple or book. Nor does the brain send out any projections to properly adjudicate the presence or the qualities of that apple: just more and different neurons connecting to one another. Despite efforts to reduce the mind to the brain (Churchland 1989) or to eliminate the mind altogether, we readily and determinedly behave as if we were and are correctly seeing (sensing) the world. That conviction is what allows us to be naïve, inasmuch as the mystery of how those electrochemical happenings can and do fool us into thinking we are objective observers of the world remains as such: a mystery that we happily choose to forget. No matter how much we are in error, we continue to convince ourselves of our objectivity. That is our naïveté.

This detour should allow us to see that everything that we see and know is surely locked inside our skull and so, in that limited sense, is all owned by us. No matter how it got there, the contents of the brain now reside in the bony appendage, the skull. We may have been taught the alphabet by a teacher, or instructed in proper manners by our mother, or even born with a host of unconscious fantasies; but, for now, they all belong to us and travel with us. It is, of course, a grave mistake to say that inasmuch as our knowledge of the apple is a conglomeration of electrochemical activity, the psychological existence of the apple is a fiction (Dennett 1991). But it is an equally absurd error to say that the apple is not physically there at all. At a minimum, we are forced to consider the idea that this locked-in brain seems not to be coexistent with the mind, that we routinely act and think as if we are in an open exchange with the things of the world; thus, we would be forced to admit that the apple sitting in the grocery window is certainly not owned by us, all the while recognizing that the entire grocery is likewise just a new set of neuronal activity moving along in our brain. Therefore, whether or not everything is in the brain and owned by us alone, we recognize that not everything in the mind should be understood by the concept of ownership. We need to better situate the mind.

The Psyche

Since Freud was a naïve realist, he needed to construct the boundaries of what he studied by building a model, which he initially derived from the physical limitations of the brain. He suggested different sorts of neurons and different forms of excitation as he struggled to move between the neurological and the psychological (S. Freud 1895). He was convinced that we lived both in an internal world, which he called the psyche, and an external world out there, outside of our skin. All of the modifications of his psychic models, from the topographic to the structural (S. Freud 1923), were based on this two-world premise, and this concept was carried forth by the influential essay on the representational world (Sandler and Rosenblatt 1962) as well as the popular book *The Self and the Object World* by Jacobson (1964). This work has nicely culminated in the definition offered by Moore and Fine that a representation is "a more or less consistent reproduction within the mind of a perception of a meaningful thing or object" (1990, 166). Now this is surely the doctrine of naïve realism, which assumes that the brain is a camera whose productions are viewed by the mind, which, in turn, is some form of internal record. The main points here are not only that there are no miniature things in the mind, but also the conviction that we do accurately reproduce the world. That is really an act of faith.

It is unclear as to the exact point at which Freud's encapsulated model needed to be altered to accommodate the external environment, but this revised version certainly became dominant with the efforts of the ego psychologists to emphasize how the function of the ego was to adapt to this outer world (Hartmann 1939). The only recourse one had with the extant models was to replicate the external world in a manner suggested by Moore and Fine. Of course, that apple outside is *not* reproduced inside, inasmuch as the only apple we can know is the one that is mysteriously created by the electrochemical activity of the brain. That process, called phenomenology by the philosophers, is not a process of bringing the outer world inside as much as we would like to believe it is. It is essentially the way we are able to experience whatever is out there. These experiences are simply all that we have, like it or not. It *is* the world, or at least it is *our* world.

Not surprisingly, all sorts of philosophers have jumped in to solve this mind/brain dilemma or mystery. And also without surprise, for the most part, they also subscribe to the seemingly unsolvable dilemma that involves a wholesale transfer of the stuff of the outside world to a place inside, where it can be examined by way of its representations. Such a transfer, conveniently dubbed the representational theory of the mind, is felt by some to be a solution, while for others it is simply a displacement of the problem. It is not clear why the apples of the world are better situated in the electrochemical activity that we declare depicts what lies outside of us, than in the electrochemical activity we decide is situated inside of us, that is, the psyche. It is a division that we embrace as fact.

According to the neurologist W. J. Freeman (2000), there are no copies or representations of the external world—there is only activity creating individual meaningful perceptions, and mine can never be the same as yours. His data also show that there can be no lasting copies, because sensory data are immediately washed away and the entire brain takes over, creating new percepts for every experience. That conclusion is not one that is readily accepted, as true as it may be. We seem to insist upon the divide between inner and outer, and as psychoanalysis developed, the problem of representations seemed to grow. The representational theory of the mind has long dominated analytic thinking and has locked us into the duality of Moore and Fine, a duality based on the need to match the perception with a stored copy.

I shall not review the host of philosophical struggles with this divide problem, but philosophers from Immanuel Kant (1781) to John McDowell (1994) to Hilary Putnam (1999) have patiently explained to us how the mind and the world are connected, all the while subscribing to the boundary that they accept as dividing these two entities. Kant felt that we know things only through our sense perceptions, which alone determine how we come to learn about things; and thus these things or phenomena are "appearances," while the "thing in itself" can never be known. Trying to go beyond appearance caused problems as McDowell expanded on this Kantian view in his claim of openness to the world. Yet he remained wedded to the division. Putnam reviewed the many efforts to conceptualize perceptual experiences without an interface between us and the world (1999, p. 1689). His best answer was a reference to John Dewey, who said, "Mind is primarily a verb. It denotes all the ways in which we deal consciously and expressly with the situations in which we find ourselves. Unfortunately, an influential manner of thinking has changed modes of action into an underlying substance that performs the activities in questions. It has treated mind as an independent entity which attends, purposes, cares and remembers" (Dewey [1934] 1991, 268). Putnam pleads for an alternative to the viewpoint that turns to "underlying substances" and that regularly invokes the brain.

If we join with Putnam in a search for alternatives, we should recognize that we cannot merely adopt Dewey's suggestion, as cogent as it is, since we must also remain faithful to the Freudian contribution of the unconscious. We cannot allow our concept of mind to merely remain on a level of discourse between conscious persons. We must navigate between the subpersonal or neurologic and the social psychological phenomenology of many nonpsychoanalytic psychologies. Psychoanalysis sits between the two. Psychoanalysis should try to utilize new metaphors that allow an escape from the restrictions imposed by reducing the mind to a small space within the skull, and yet that resist a superficial trend which can result from a focus on the conscious relationship. Although the majority of analysts are quite flexible in their conceptualizations of these conundrums, the suggestion of a different metaphor may lend a certain clarity to these issues. The following is one trial of a new metaphor.

Owning

An analyst reported a patient entering his office and immediately rearranging the chairs as well as the vase of flowers on a table. The analyst felt mildly annoyed that his "space" was being invaded, but he felt that it was of little moment and so could be readily allowed. The listening group of clinicians to which he reported this case had a mixed reaction ranging from simple dismissal of the issue to a firm declaration that this sort of personal invasion should not be allowed. A few felt that such acting-in demonstrated a certain form of pathology in the patient and argued as to whether it should be ignored or attended to. The patient had overstepped a boundary, not one of ethical significance, but rather one of psychological import. All sorts of meaning could be attached to this action, which demanded some connection to an unconscious motive. No matter if the patient insisted that the chairs and flowers looked better in their new sites—the assembled group read the moves as indicating a hidden motive of a patient behaving as if she owned the space.

This issue of ownership, rather easily observed in an overt action, carries over into the arena where most of analysis takes place. It is representative of the placement of a personal stamp upon some thing or some idea. It is able to be conceptualized as an expansion of the self to include or incorporate that thing or idea. It is an act of the mind as a verb.

Own is a verb. It should allow us an opportunity to see if it is of some use in better conceptualizing the invasion of space felt by this therapist whose patient rearranged his furniture. This supposed space of his need not be transposed to a place in order to pursue this investigation. The therapist would probably agree that there was a gradation of ownership in his reckoning, in that he surely might not allow another person to make an alteration in his clothing or his hair or even the chair in which he sat. He felt less concerned about her moving her chair and perhaps even less about those flowers in the vase. He can easily classify his feelings of possession in some quantitative way that seems more appropriate than a simple division of being in or out of his mind. And one could also see that different people might feel differently about each of those items. It is also possible to draw a line at which one's claim of ownership drops off completely. So, too, can one probably delineate an area where shared ownership seems probable and allowable. However, sharing is also something that is quantifiable in a relative way, and this assignment of quantity opens the door to a consideration of unconscious motives. We know that all of the possessions in an office have a significance that is wrapped up in feelings that we have about our chairs, our vases, and our personal clothing. The next step is to better focus the concept of ownership on what is regularly felt to be the heart of psychoanalysis. Then we can begin to see the range of owning that covers location, possession, and agency.

Owning the Transference

It would seem to be without contradiction that today's ideas about transference no longer make the claim that it is a pure misperception of the analyst by the patient. The idea of mutual participation is insisted upon by a number of analysts (Hoffman 1994) who rarely go so far as to properly apportion the respective percentage of input by the involved parties, but rather seem primarily interested in the recognition of the analyst's inability to be neutral. The desire of the patient is always met by the desire of the analyst. Thus, the transference belongs to both, and we see an opportunity to examine ownership in terms of possession. Consideration of the ownership of countertransference will be addressed briefly later in this chapter and in more detail in chapter 9.

Case Illustration

An analytic patient announced a schedule conflict with a session the following week and talked about possibly canceling his appointment. As the time approached he decided to attend at the regular time, and on the day of his analytic hour he reported a dream in which he was with a man who was crowding him and not giving him enough room to do his job. The patient's associations easily led to his feeling about somehow being compelled or expected to keep his appointment. He then proceeded to discuss the many places in his life where he had to live up to other people's expectations for him and how angry these demands made him. He also spoke of how much it pleased him to perform well and so to live up to what people would expect from him. I, as analyst, readily recognized my pleasure at the patient's decision to keep his appointment, and I could in no way deny that the patient might somehow have picked up on and so recognized my own desire. It should be clear that in one sense the appointment(s) belonged to both of us.

This mutual construction easily involves the conclusion that there was shared ownership of the event of the patient's keeping the appointment. Whatever was in the patient's mind joined with something in mine to produce his presence. However, it must go beyond the conscious level of the relationship to enable us to demonstrate a psychoanalytic ownership. It is here that we can approach an answer to the question of who owns the transference; accordingly, we might apply the same analysis to the issue of countertransference.

Depending on what theoretical tool is employed, different analysts will pursue different avenues to extract what they believe to be the essentials of the transference. Each pursuit will aim to make the behavior of the patient as well as his reported dream intelligible. That is to say, the decision of this patient to come to the analytic hour followed by the angry dream are actions that go beyond the agreed-upon coconstruction of a narrative to motives that are not readily apparent and/or are arrived at only by undoing an analytic defense or resistance. In this particular patient, with my particular outlook, we together explained the behavior and dream as derived from a childhood characterized by the patient's being treated as a special child who often, but not always, was expected to shine and perform beyond the abilities of his siblings and his peers, and perhaps even beyond his own wishes.

No matter how much one agrees with this formulation or how many alternative explanations may be offered, it is possible at this point to assign a weight to the contribution of the patient along with that of the analyst. My feeling was that this particular psychological configuration arose primarily, if not exclusively, from the patient's autobiographical contribution, and thus this was transference material primarily owned by the patient and responded to by me. Such conclusions are routinely subject to qualifications and second-guessing, but that discussion is not the subject of this effort. What is hoped for is a clearer grasp of the ownership of the transference, that goes beyond the *potential* superficiality of simply suggesting a relationship as interpersonal or intersubjective. In the lexicon, for instance, of self psychology the analyst had become the self object asked to mirror a childhood grandiosity that repeated an angry reaction to demands that could not comfortably be met. Other theories can form a different explanation with a different vocabulary, but absent some form of unconscious material the resulting story is not tantamount to a psychoanalytic explanation.

It should be noted here that the transference which we scrutinize and study is not a thing that resides in a place, but something better considered as a concept that is capable of possession. Ideas do not necessarily have a home, although they are often so designated. It is an option as to whether one assigns ideas to a space or location or assigns them a power. Transference is an idea that can be thought of in a variety of ways, but if we insist that it lives inside of one or another person, we may well be trapped in our thinking. All of the conveniences of (say) projection or internalization are accompanied by the companion inconveniences of wondering just how an idea travels from my brain to yours or manages to take up a place inside of me. That puzzle of internal travel is never to be solved. Rather, it should be dismissed as unlikely.

Owning the Countertransference

An analytic patient somewhere in the middle of her first year of analysis wondered if the analyst was taking notes and asked him to stop. She said that she was very sensitive to the idea of being used or exploited and wished that her analysis be for her and her alone. Thus she wanted no notes or record of her case, no presentation of her case to colleagues with the single exception of a supervising analyst if need be, and certainly no publication of her case in any book or journal. When this problem was reported to a group, the responses ranged from those insisting upon respecting the desire of the patient to those that suggested the patient be told that this demand could not be met, so that it might be wise to choose another analyst if the problem could not be solved in this one.

In this particular case, the analyst felt that his own unconscious thoughts and feelings about the patient which arose before her injunction about note-taking were important enough for scientific dissemination.[1] He had discussed this with a supervisor, who urged him to write up and present the case. When the patient declared her opposition to this possibility, the analyst was stymied. He had not begun this analysis with her consent for publication, and he wondered if he could continue it in his present state of frustration: a conscious and disagreeable one. It was clear to him that the narrative of and about the patient was her property, and that he could lay no claim to it. Yet he strongly felt that his own ideas about the case—the conscious ones that enabled him to formulate and follow the material, plus the newly discovered unconscious ones that he had talked over with his supervisor—seemed to belong to him. Although everyone agreed that this was an issue that merited discussion and possible analysis, the facts of the case were those of an impasse rather than of a resolution.

The aforementioned analyst felt that he could in no way write up and present his countertransference feelings about his patient without her recognition of the case, no matter how effectively he might disguise it from others who might recognize her. He also felt quite strongly that all analysts learn things from patients which they can make effective use of in the treatment of future cases, and so this particular patient's insistence that she and she alone be the beneficiary of this analysis could not be met. But most strongly, he was convinced that he owned his own countertransference and that he should be free to distribute or disseminate it as he saw fit. He did not feel that it was a product of a coconstruction or even a proper element of the patient's narrative. It was his.

A case report (expanded upon in the following chapter and also discussed in chapter 4) in the *Journal of Clinical Ethics* (Jaffe 2003) examines the reactions of a patient who discovered a report of his psychiatric treatment in a journal, a report that upset him greatly because of what the therapist reported about his own feelings about the patient. Although this patient

---

1. The wholesale use of the word *countertransference* to cover the entirety of an analyst's reactions, ranging from his conscious feelings, to his own transferences to the patient, to his countertransferences which are initially unconscious, is not a use that can be easily dismissed.

had given permission to have his case published, he had done so long before this discovery of its publication, and now could barely remember having done so. He was enraged at his reading, and the journal presents the patient's reaction along with commentary from a number of ethicists, all of whom agree that the protection of the patient is paramount.

Without by any means offering to solve what is properly considered as either a moral or an ethical dilemma, it may be possible to clarify the nature of some psychological problems by posing them as struggles over possession. So, too, can some new understanding be gained by efforts to transpose fixed modes of how we see things into different arenas or by employing new metaphors. The concept of ownership includes that of agency, that is, the one who initiates and controls action (Schafer 1976). The agent becomes the owner, inasmuch as he or she makes the decisions as to what and when these actions are to take place. In psychoanalysis the self is a better concept or model to handle the issues such as placing one's stamp upon acts, while the ego as executor seems to leave the issue of ownership to the side. These niceties of theory are, however, not paramount, since we are aiming for clarity of explanation. It is useful to go beyond the specific points of transference and countertransference to see if the use of owning and ownership as a working tool can shed light on other points of clinical interest. The next example is one directed at a patient's conflict that is revisited with the new tool involving agency.

Case Illustration

A patient in psychotherapy had accumulated an overabundance of luxury clothing and accessories which jammed her closets and led her to financial ruin. Directed to go into treatment by others because the addiction to shopping had become uncontrollable, her associated depression as well as the rage of her family initially took center stage in her treatment. However, not too long after the onset of therapy, the patient confessed that she hardly ever wore any of the clothes or accessories and, indeed, probably had duplicates of many of them. She was stirred by their beauty and unable to resist possessing them. No matter how remorseful she may have been after a purchase, she could never bring herself to return the items. Sometimes she looked at them, but never for long.

I shall now go into the particulars of the clinical process, but ask your indulgence in acknowledging that these articles of expensive and special significance were revealed to be representatives of the patient's self. I should now clarify that the term *representation* is used to refer to propositions or images that are internal to the mind as well as those considered external to the mind. The first category of representation is divided into the denotation of specific objects as well as more symbolic concepts. The second category refers to public phenomena such as pictures or icons. For us to move a step beyond the internal-external dichotomy, we may safely say that the beautiful boots and jackets were all felt by the patient to be stand-ins for her self, and so they stood for something both exceptional and hidden from view. This thumbnail sketch was formulated to be emblematic of much that was significant in the patient's childhood.

After a good deal of therapeutic work dealing with this woman's struggle over the emergence and recognition of her own grandiose exhibitionism, she announced one day that she was beginning to empty out her closets and to sell off their contents. Each and every piece was carefully lifted out, examined, and marveled over. And, perhaps not surprisingly, the process was not one of mourning but rather was associated with a heretofore-unexperienced sense of freedom. The clothing that she had once owned was no longer owned; in its place she owned a different self configuration that was now invigorated with the unconscious grandiosity once kept hidden in the closets and drawers of her home. It is interesting to conceptualize the movement of possession from the luxury items owned by the self to the newly formed self. This self, now without crammed closets, can be described through any number of psychoanalytic models and theories. We certainly need to have a meaningful way to consider the difference between my automobile, my haircut, and myself that carries more information than a mere assignment of position and place. There does seem to be an added richness to the story of this patient when we center it in the process of owning and relinquishing. So, too, can we follow the subtly different functions of the word *own*.

Discussion

Spatial metaphors dominate psychoanalysis. Once one begins to think in terms of "in" and "out," one constructs an area with a boundary, hence the concepts of inside and outside. The transition from "in the brain" to "in the mind" follows easily, and along with these concepts the use of *internal* and *external* comes naturally. Thus we speak of projection as if a thought travels from one mind to another, and of internalization as if one digests a feeling just as one eats a sandwich.

The move away from spatial metaphors should not be difficult. For instance, we readily agree that sin is a problem in many religions without a worry as to where to locate sin. When it comes to objects or things or persons, however, we seem to allow the dimensions of the physical entity to determine its contents. In a way, we become prisoners of our language (Nehamas 1985) as well as of our visions. Thus, when we postulate a self in psychoanalysis, we seem to take it for granted that it is the same self as seen and used in sociology or physiology or even in advertising. We forget that the data of analysis probably require a different concept of a self and possibly even one that ignores the natural boundary of the skin. William James said that one's self included one's possessions up to and including one's horse. Thus for him and perhaps for psychoanalysis, the concept of ownership casts a wider net than one encased by the skin (James 1950).

Once freed from spatial metaphors, we face a danger of trafficking in themes of social relationships. Since Freud was so apt to illustrate his ideas as existing in areas of significance, we seem to feel that in our fidelity to him, we must maintain similar areas. We speak of the contents of the id and superego as if they were packages that could be opened and examined (Brenman Pick 1985). If we put these packages aside, we may momentarily forget to account for, or lose sight of, the unconscious and move to "relationships" as if telling a story or writing a play. One answer to the dual dangers of superficiality and bounded entities is the employment of other theoretical words such as ownership. As I hoped to illustrate in the last clinical example, a patient may find her self in her jewelry and apparel, and its concealment may have a hidden meaning to be unlocked only by an analytic form of inquiry. This joins the unconscious with action in and of the world.

Summary and Conclusions

This is an exercise in the employment of different ways of thinking and talking about the mind, an exercise that takes a step away from the mind as a repository of thoughts and feelings. Using the concept of ownership and stressing the mind as primarily a verb of action, the examination of various facets of psychic functioning is undertaken. Owning can be understood as covering issues of location regarding whether the contents of the mind are within the brain; of possession regarding whether the owner of transference and countertransference is the patient or the analyst; and of agency regarding the self configuration that initiates action. This exercise is directed toward a solution and resolution of seemingly insurmountable struggles in psychoanalysis such as that of the intrapsychic versus the interpersonal, which can best be seen as problems of language rather than of ideas.

One argument that is presented to the problems resulting from the metaphors that we employ is that they are merely ways of speaking. Unfortunately, they also become ways of thinking, which then become points of disagreement, argument, and dissension. A step away from the struggle allows us to see these disagreements as capable of resolution by the employment of new and different ways of speaking.

CHAPTER NINE

Who Owns the Countertransference?

A recent series of articles published in the *Journal of Clinical Ethics* (Jaffe 2003) and noted in the previous chapter presents a published case study of a patient in psychotherapy along with the responses of a number of readers, including a response from the patient himself. The basic point of these essays has to do with the patient's consent for the publication of his case and the repercussions that ensued from his reading about himself from his psychiatrist's point of view. The report included a good deal of the psychiatrist's feelings about treating this patient, feelings that he had never previously shared with his patient and that turned out to be quite hurtful to the patient. Although the patient had given his consent to have his case published, this consent had been agreed to long before the case had been written up; and indeed, the patient hardly remembered that moment of agreement until presented with the finished product. The journal included essays by both the psychiatrist and the patient, with discussions by a number of ethicists who themselves seem quite committed to the dual task of allowing a patient to read what is said about him while ensuring that this will not be harmful or injurious to him. Most readers will probably conclude that the delicate effort at a balanced approach to the problem has not resulted in a happy solution.

Some Background

I shall not review the extensive literature on confidentiality of psychoanalytic publications, which has been adequately reviewed and discussed by Gabbard (2000) and Galatzer-Levy (2003). Rather, I wish to pose our particular dilemma as one between the stance of the International Committee of Medical Journal Editors (1995) and that of the Committee on Scientific

Activities of the American Psychoanalytic Association (1984). The guide-lines of the first say that published information must "be essential for scientific purposes," and "the patient or proxy must give written informed consent for publication." These statements have the form of a law and are decisive. The second group does not demand consent but leaves it up to the author to protect the patient. Protection ranges from alteration or omis-sion of material to thick disguise of the patient. The latter usually demands that no one other than the patient can recognize himself as the one being written about. This takes the form of a calculation and a judgment. Each of these positions centers its attention on patient protection and gives the vulnerable patient the maximum concern, yet each has a status of its own and is really in opposition to the other.

Ownership

The crux of the issue of revealing something about the treatment of a pa-tient often comes down to a question of ownership. Although the property status of human tissue is controversial (National Bioethics Advisory Com-mittee 1999), the *Journal of Clinical Ethics* states that patients clearly have ownership of their stories (Jaffe 2003) and so lay claim to privacy.

The narrative constructed in the formation and presentation of a case history is felt to belong solely to the patient, who must either give per-mission for its distribution or else be protected from any harm that could result from its publication. Thus, on one end of an imaginary line that we would construct, we would have the treatment, whether psychoanalysis or psychotherapy, as an activity done solely for the benefit of the patient, with all attendant issues, such as property rights, belonging to the patient. Midway on our imagined axis we could fashion a coconstructed narrative that is a product of two authors as well as an entity that would allow for a claim of dual or shared ownership. Finally, at the opposite pole of patient ownership, there could be a point that seems to belong in its entirety to the therapist.

It is often a poor analogy to place physical medicine alongside psycho-logic treatment, but we surely can agree that (say) a surgical technique that is honed and perfected on one or more patients should be freely available to future patients. That technique or knowledge has become the property of the surgeon, with due gratitude to the patients who lent themselves to its development. So, too, in psychotherapy and psychoanalysis, each patient is a potential laboratory to develop our own skills until, over time, these become so much a part of a practitioner that she is hard-pressed to identify their origins. The fuzziness begins in the middle; only at the extremes does clarity ensue.

Case Illustration

An interesting case in analysis presented a bit of clinical material which I felt had heretofore not been represented in the literature. I wrote up the case, including the major pertinent issues having to deal with my counter-transference reactions to the clinical material. I showed the written up case to a consultant who felt that it was a significant contribution that ought to be published. The wisdom of this conclusion is not the issue here, but the dilemma is. In truth the value of most contributions is determined over time and cannot be readily apparent. Although the identity of the individual in the case could be disguised from everyone but the patient, it could certainly not be so concealed from the patient. If he or she would read of my countertransference reactions, it seemed to me to be potentially harmful to the conduct of the analysis. Nor could I show the written case to the patient for consent to publish, since it might readily recapitulate the sad events written up in the aforementioned journal. In the latter case, the hurt and angry patient did return to his therapist to work out the derailment caused by his reading of the case, and the therapist felt that both he and the patient had profited from this unfortunate circumstance. It seems, then, that the harm can come at any time, even after termination. But one can hardly make a case for the supposed ameliorative effects of a return being universally true. Stoller's (1988) advice is to let all patients edit and disguise their own cases, but it is given in the form of a universal rule, and I had no doubt whatsoever that it would not apply to my patient and my countertransference. Nor was I eager to test my conclusion. Rightly or wrongly, I felt that thick disguise would destroy the point I wished to make, and I saw no way out. No solution seemed to fit.

Discussion

The benefit of the case presented in the *Journal of Clinical Ethics* is that for the most part, it represents a situation in which everyone would have been better off if the writeups had never been seen by the patient. Of course the best but not the only way to achieve this is never to publish anything save fiction or theory. Many potential but unwilling writers or those who simply cannot write take refuge behind this solution. Indeed, one often finds that the most zealous defenders of patient protection come from the ranks of the nonwriters. The other solutions available to solve the dilemma are nicely listed and discussed by Galatzer-Levy (2003), but he shows them all to have their own failings. In fact, he concludes his article and joins with Gabbard by stating that all supposed solutions face difficulties.

If we move away from the very valuable point devoted to patient protection and patient ownership, we may arrive closer to one of therapist ownership, as in my countertransference, coupled with a possible benefit to future patients. The risk is clear. The answer is less so, but not beyond us. It begins with our dispensing with a commitment to any set of rules that govern all case presentations and publications. If we embrace pragmatism, then we need to recognize that some patients should indeed be consulted beforehand, some disguised minimally, some disguised thickly, and perhaps some disguised not at all. Stoller (1988) may have carved out a group of patients who can edit their own cases, while others may delineate those who should never have to reckon with such publication. There is a grave danger in treating all patients alike as well as in taking for granted a higher moral code to which we must all conform.

When Gabbard states that no approach is without its problems, he argues that a clinical decision must be made in each case regarding whether it is the best strategy to use thick disguise, to ask the patient's consent, to limit the clinical illustration to process data without biographical details, to ask a colleague to serve as author, or to use composites. Once again the goal is to minimize the potential harm to the patient while maximizing the scientific value of the contribution (Gabbard 2000). Those are excellent guidelines, but the above-noted journal case and my own quandary seem to suggest that there is simply no way to know the best strategy beforehand, no guarantee of achieving the goal anticipated by Gabbard. Not only is no approach without its problems, but the potential problem usually is not readily apparent in making one's clinical decision. Can it be that we cannot write without risk?

There is an interesting discussion by Derrida on ethical decisions in which he affirms that every such decision requires confronting its essential irreducible undecidability. John Caputo summarizes Derrida's point: "The opposite of 'undecidability' is not decisiveness but is calculability. Decision-making, judgment, on the other hand, positively depends upon undecidability. So, a 'just' decision, a 'judgment' that is worthy of its name, one that responds to the demands of justice, one that is more than merely legal, goes eyeball to eyeball with undecidability, stares it in the face (literally), looks into that abyss, and then makes the leap, that is, 'gives itself up to the impossible decision'" (1997, 137). Alas, just as psychoanalysis is one of the impossible professions, it also is burdened with impossible decisions.

Conclusion

Most ethicists and moralists aim to form laws of behavior that cover all persons, such as embodied in the Golden Rule of doing unto others as you would have them do unto you. However, most persons decide their behavior on a more pragmatic, ad hoc basis, and this may well result in behavior that ranges from the utterly selfish to the most altruistic. What psychoanalysts have learned is that all behavior is complex, much of it unconscious, and so we are more often befuddled than confident about the meaning of behavior. Ethicists who promulgate universal rules may indeed do us more harm than good. Absolutes in psychoanalysis and psychotherapy are conveniences that can inhibit and blind us. We may profit more from devoting some time to better categorizing our patients as either those who may not care at all if they are presented as case material, those who care just enough to be disguised, those who would give consent if they could edit the case, or those who would forbid any sort of publication. This is not meant as a solution but could lead to a better clarification of the dilemma. As I have observed earlier, it may simply not be true that confidentiality is an absolute privilege that must always be observed, or that privacy is a fundamental right of all patients. Rather, confidentiality and privacy may be proper objects of investigation, investigations that are waylaid by those who would claim certainty about the right way to behave.

The investigations that are necessary to better equip us to make a proper determination about privacy and confidentiality are probably not those that divide therapists and analysts as to their preferred procedures. As interesting as that research may be, it is not of paramount importance. What is needed is a clearer idea of how we balance the risk of disclosure with the need for disclosure. Both patient and therapist should enjoy rights to attain this balance. Analyses are coconstructions and lend value to each of the participants. We surely cannot create a risk-free answer while maintaining our credibility as scientists. Obligations and ownership go both ways.

PART THREE

The Contingency of Correct Behavior

CHAPTER TEN

Another Look at Neutrality

A newspaper report (*New York Times*, April 19, 2005, p. A9) quoted a Catholic cardinal delivering a homily that warned against deviation from tradition. He said, "A dictatorship of relativism recognizes nothing as definite and which leaves as the ultimate measure only one's ego and desires. . . . Relativism, that is letting oneself be carried here and there by any wind of doctrine, appears with the sole attitude good enough for modern times." This dichotomy of relativism versus foundationalism may be misleading, and this is revealed by an examination of how we use language to speak about the two. Language relates to the world in three ways: The first implies a one-to-one correspondence between the world and the word. The word is a surrogate for the referent, and as we saw in chapter 8, some analytic theory does indeed adopt this viewpoint. The second connection between language and the world links it to mental states such as images and perceptions. A majority of analysts do ascribe to this viewpoint. The third breaks the link between word and world by seeing language, as we noted earlier in reference to Oakeshott, as validated by usages of language communities. Best said by Roy Harris (2005) in speaking of history but also true of language and possibly of morals, language is a nonstop process of contextualization and recontextualization in a multiplicity of ways and a multiplicity of settings for a multiplicity of audiences.

In contrast with the cardinal who both knew and insisted upon the truth, we see that truth is context sensitive and must include the participants who fashion it in the context of that enterprise. If we were able to have a one-to-one correspondence between words or images and the world, we might also be able to achieve the neutral place to stand. If, however, we cannot escape context, neutrality may be unattainable. To ask an analyst to assume a neutral stance is a challenge that can be addressed by an initial inquiry into what the word means.

Webster's Third International Dictionary defines *neutrality* as "a condition of being uninvolved in contests or controversies between others or refraining from taking part on either side of such contest or controversy." There is some disagreement as to whether Freud ever actually used the word *neutrality*. In his "Observations on Transference Love," he is said to have written: "In my opinion, therefore, we ought not to give up the neutrality toward the patient" (S. Freud [1915] 1953–74, 12:164); however, the German word *indifferenz* is translated by Strachey as "neutrality" rather than "indifference." Jorge Canestri, for one, feels indifference is harsher than neutrality but has an advantage in that it corresponds to "an attitude of equal availability, a uniformly spread attention, distributed without distinction over all the 'material' presented by the patient" (1993, 150–51). Nevertheless, Strachey's translated word has survived.

Anna Freud presents her definition of *neutrality* by stating: "He (the analyst) directs his attention equally and objectively to the unconscious element in all three institutions. To put it another way, when he sets about the work of enlightenment he takes his stand at a point equidistant from the id, the ego, and the superego" (1946, 30). I take this to mean that the analyst's place is equidistant from those institutions of the patient rather than those of himself. This and other definitions are commonly combined with the principle of abstinence, which, according to Eickhoff, "is manifestly linked with neutrality, which signifies a Utopian ideal of impartiality and noninterference, the analyst's aim not to become a real character in the life of the patient. It is connected in the closest possible way with the values implicit in the analytic attitude, the ethic of truthfulness, respect for freedom of thought, and the therapeutic aim of psychoanalysis, to handle the most dangerous mental impulses and to obtain mastery over them for the benefit of the patient" (1993, 50).

In pursuing this connection between these principles of neutrality and abstinence and that of values, Sigmund Freud said, "From the point of view of morality, the control and restriction of instinct, it may be said of the id that it is totally non-moral, of the ego that it strives to be moral, and of the super-ego that it can be hyper-moral and then become as ruthless as only the id can be" ([1923] 1953–54, 19:54).

Fifty years after these words were published, Gabbard, in regard to abstinence and neutrality, writes:

These metapsychological constructs are difficult for a therapist to locate, however, and putting the definition into action may be a formidable challenge. The underlying principle, which is still valid to some degree, is that a psychodynamic therapist tries to remain nonjudgmental. . . .

One of the major difficulties in implementing a nonjudgmental atmosphere in psychotherapy is that therapists are privately passing judgments on patients all the time. (2003, 60)

If one compares the dictionary definition of *neutrality* with its protean psychoanalytic and psychotherapeutic journey, there seem to be a number of crucial differences between being uninvolved or indifferent from that of being able to direct one's attention to unconscious elements in all three institutions. If one is to be aware of and stay connected to the values implicit in the analytic attitude, along with being aware of the analyst's private thoughts and personal values, the task seems formidable.

In his discussion of "active technique," which involves exploiting the transference rather than analyzing it, Glover tells us that Freud was ready to adapt or modify technique according to the case. Also, he says that confusion has reigned over the issue of neutrality, and that there is no unanimity on the amount of interference included in "correct analysis." He goes on to say that "complete neutrality" is a myth (Glover 1958, 170). Of course, this conclusion opens the question as to whether there can be any validity at all to the question of neutrality, and whether the introduction of "active technique" was the result of the rather mythological status of neutrality. Indeed, Glover (p. 136) also talks of neutrality as a defense when he describes patients who copy the policy of the analyst and so do not allow emotional reactions of any kind into the analysis, as was illustrated above by Lander in chapter 5, on confidentiality. The majority of writers on this topic say that the difficulties in attaining a neutral stance arise from influences stemming from the patient that in turn lead to an interference in the analyst's capacity to objectively evaluate the patient: the behavior of the analyst in departing from a position of neutrality has been rationalized by some to warrant and promote the newly anointed "active technique."

The equidistance championed by Anna Freud can be said to apply to the analyst who stands equidistant from both the patient's id, ego, and superego as well as from his own psychic agencies. In the former the analyst is positioned as "a telephone receiver to a transmitting microphone" (S. Freud [1912] 1953–74, 12:115–16), while in the latter the analyst must attain neutrality "through the control of the countertransference" (Canestri 1993,

150). These activities seem better visualized as two microphones talking and two transmitters receiving.

To return to the idea of indifference, not only is it harsher than neutrality, but it also evokes a quite different meaning, one of not caring— something earlier discussed in chapter 6, on thoughtlessness. If something matters not at all to you, you are indifferent. If, however, you are torn between alternative matters, you may care deeply, but a balance may exist that can perhaps constitute neutrality. The analyst or therapist who satisfies Anna Freud's concept of equidistance is probably best thought of as having achieved a balance between opposing forces, forces formed by both the patient's and the therapist's psychic agencies. The following is an example that challenges that concept.

Case Illustration

Chris came into treatment as a very tense and pressured young man who immediately confessed that he felt it imperative to do something about his addiction to Internet pornography. He was spending more and more time on a variety of pornographic sites, which he said were of more and more disturbing and even pathological content. He would masturbate while watching, and only after his ejaculating would he be able to stop for a while until drawn back to the activity once again.

Chris was a married father of two boys and insisted that he was happily married to a woman who had no idea whatsoever of his secret life. I will not describe the treatment in detail, but rather will describe the nature of my struggle to achieve neutrality or perhaps of my failure to do so because of caring.

Shortly after entering into treatment, Chris reported an enormous sense of relief and an accompanying cessation of his pornography preoccupation. My initial reaction to the details of this symptom was a combination of excitement along with compassion for this patient, who seemed genuinely troubled by what we agreed was an uncontrollable addiction. When he reported the very positive reaction to his entering treatment, I felt both pleased and silently powerful. My theoretical formulation for this sudden segue into success was that I had been assigned a place in the psychic structure of the patient. I had temporarily become a sort of superego surrogate, which lent the patient a sense of control and regulation. Both Chris and I were pleased at this rapid move to symptom relief, and we joined in the hope that this would be more than an evanescent experience.

I think it fair to say that I was neither indifferent to my patient's plight nor neutral about his initial rapid improvement. Of course, I was able to inhibit any overt expression of my "private thoughts and personal values" and so to satisfy the portrait of neutrality. However, it seems evident that the stance recommended by Anna Freud was in no way applicable to my relationship with my patient. One might say that she was referring to a different sort of patient, or to a different phase in the treatment or analysis of such a patient. Perhaps this was due to a failure of mine to properly conceptualize how I could indeed manage to be equidistant from id, ego, and superego while simultaneously occupying a locus for his superego.

If I contemplate Glover's differentiation of "active technique," I might be able to see myself as "exploiting the transference," but that would be a difficult challenge to support, inasmuch as I could scarcely admit to any activity whatsoever. My theoretical formulation led me to believe that Chris had at one time experienced the kind of superego activity that I felt I now represented. In a greatly oversimplified way, I hypothesized that Chris either was possessed of two forms of conscience that controlled or were unable to control these impulses of his, or that he somehow needed the physical and emotional presence of a parental surrogate to exercise such control. His reported happy marriage indicated that only a very particular configuration of the "other" was required that would provide adequate self-control. I might well have been advised at this initial stage of Chris's treatment to refrain from revealing any evaluation of my own as to his temporarily (we assumed) achieved improvement, and I could well see how I could join with neither his victory over his impulses nor his fear of their ultimate reappearance.

This seems to suggest two forms of neutrality: the one that lends itself to the poker face of restraint in the analyst as seen by the patient, and the other that jockeys for a balance in the analyst's countertransference. One must, however, add the moral component to this mix, since Chris and I seemed to have implicitly agreed that his pornographic preoccupation was an immoral activity that was only to be condemned. The preoccupation did have something in common with any symptom such as compulsive hand washing or depression, but one could not dismiss the added component of its being thought of as fundamentally wrong. Although other formulations may be entertained, I did not feel that Chris had the "flight into health" that is sometimes seen in patients who cannot allow the regression required to properly gain insight into their problems. Rather, it seemed that entering treatment allowed him to attain an added psychological structure that served to strengthen his ability to further examine his unfortunate state, at least for a while.

If Chris and I were to enjoy together his newly found relief from the urgency of his pornographic addiction, it would best be explained by my forming an empathic connection with him. So, too, would the return of this problem require of me a similar sort of empathy. Thus, what was asked of me for a proper therapeutic stance would be a momentary embrace of an essentially immoral posture. And in recognition of Sigmund Freud's comment about values, I would then be closer in line with the impulses of the id than those of the prohibitions of the superego.

What occurred in Chris is no different from what is seen in many similar patients who struggle with acts that are generally considered immoral. The struggle is often seen as an oscillation between desire and prohibition; these back-and-forth positions are reflective of similar moments in all of development. In terms of the respective states of the psychic institutions, one may say that either these are waxing and waning conditions in the id and superego which the ego strives to balance, or these are split and parallel configurations which gain ascendancy at one time or another. Regardless of the theoretical choice, the job of the empathic therapist would be that of experiencing a reciprocal state, thus the abandonment of any semblance of neutrality, at least for the time being (Applebaum 2005).

Achieving a Balance

Most moral concerns share a common societal position of either acceptance or prohibition. Most moral problems are solved by an appeal to one or another set of standards that have been handed down from generation to generation and form the basis of ego balance and superego prohibitions. Consequently, we are able to behave in a neutral or objective manner with patients who are caught up in moral quandaries. Most therapists would join with Chris in condemning his preoccupation with pornography, but might well be unable to fully comprehend his being drawn to this activity other than by their being able to pinpoint those moments of preoccupation and their possible causal components. To delve further into the origin and meaning of this form of behavior usually involves a temporary identification or empathic connection with the unwelcome part, an identification that must be sustained in order for the analyst to have an equivalent experience.

Imagine if you will a continuum for any particular question of morality, from complete liberty at one end to severe prohibition at the other.

Most of our societal standards cluster close together in the area of control and prohibition, while most forbidden misbehaviors occupy a position of liberty and allowance. Patients such as Chris alternate between one pole and the other and so seem to demonstrate a form of division. The capacity to understand patients such as Chris seems to require no special human traits such as honesty or integrity as much as it demands a capacity to enter into an empathic bond with these patients. The neutral stand that has often been underscored as a necessary condition for the successful treatment of such patients seems beside the point, inasmuch as the primary requirement is for anything but neutrality. Rather, what is demanded in true moral conflicts is the capacity to see both sides, and such "seeing" is never an objective or indifferent vision from outside but more of a joined experience.

One form of neutrality that seems different from that espoused by the earlier analysts quoted above is that of being truly caught in the middle of our imaginary line, of being trapped in an area of unresolvable indecision. Some moral quandaries beg for certainty but seem only to yield a balance of opposition. Whereas certainty or near-certainty is arrived at by situating oneself at or near the poles of either permission or prohibition, uncertainty is the watchword for an appeal to an outside standard of right and wrong, a standard offered by a community norm.

Experiencing a Balance

We often hear of a patient's wish to enlist us in a moral dilemma that seems not to be of much moment and toward which we may rightfully claim indifference. Of course, there is a variety of individual reactions to these trivial acts, which range from getting incorrect change and pocketing it to diminishing one's income for tax purposes, and so on and so forth. The therapist may on these occasions clearly see both sides of the dilemma and be unable to take anything like a firm stand; this type of reaction seems to qualify as a neutral stance akin to not caring very much. Here is an example.

Case Illustration

Peter was a physician in analysis whose wife was on a variety of medications. Peter had recently taken a new position at a large clinic which was visited by a number of pharmaceutical company representatives. These company employees routinely left samples of one or another drug in a closet reserved for their storage. Peter, soon after his employment, noticed that a number of drugs that his wife used and paid for were available to him for the taking, and he did so with some pleasure at saving the money that he and his wife ordinarily would pay for them. One day as he was accumulating his monthly supply, one of the other physicians commented on Peter's acquisition, and in a very matter-of-fact way said he had thought those drugs were reserved for indigent patients. When Peter reported this encounter to his analyst, he wanted very much to have his analyst's opinion as to his guilt or innocence in this activity. The analyst seemed to have no opinion and remained quiet. The next day Peter reported a dream in which he was chastised for something which later turned out to be a scolding without justification. Peter's father was representative of a man who would always try to get as much as he could out of any situation, up to and including cheating on his own siblings. Peter did not want to be anything like his dad in this regard and struggled over this current example of honesty and integrity in conflict.

Peter asked one of the other doctors about the medications in the drug closet and was told that they were considered a perk just like the free coffee, and their use for personal reasons was something everybody did. Peter's analyst could see comfortably fitting into either position according to the last person spoken to. He really had no opinion at all, and thought this a fine opportunity to objectively analyze what this all meant to Peter, especially in terms of his identification with a less than honest father. This turned out to be a fruitful part of the analysis; but over time, Peter's analyst realized that he also had no idea of just how Peter had resolved his particular dilemma, and began to wonder if perhaps his own indifference was a clue to an answer. The answer that he came up with was certainly subject to debate, because he claimed that perhaps this was not really a question of morality at all. Some people, such as the first physician, thought one way, and some, like the second, thought another way. In resolving one's identification with a parent, there is always a complex set of factors to be sorted out. No relationship is without ambivalence, and most wholesale identifications are less than satisfactory. Peter's analyst would probably think that Strachey would have served Freud best if he had translated that contested word as "indifference" rather than as "neutrality"; he felt most able to function as an analyst when he was indifferent to the issues presented as moral quandaries, which, at times, turned out to be matters of taste or preference rather than of right versus wrong.

If Peter had decided never to take drugs from the closet for personal use, he would have felt that he was a weakling submitting to a stronger authority, but his morality would be unquestioned. If he had chosen to defy this overscrupulous option, he would have felt proud but possibly corrupt. Each of these positions could be seen as corresponding to a relationship to his father, and for each he felt attraction and revulsion. And so for each he turned to his analyst for assistance and guidance, with no clear response.

Taking a Stand

There are a variety of concepts of morality, one of which is called "discourse ethics" or, more accurately, "a discourse theory of morality" developed by the German philosopher Jurgen Habermas. Its relevance here is the conviction that one must move from an individual perspective on principles and judgments to that of a shared or communicative one based on argument and interpretation. Habermas says that Kant and the categorical imperative assumed that moral validity can be adequately grasped from the perspective of an individual reflecting on his or her motives of action (Habermas 1993, xii). In contrast with this, Habermas feels that moral questions can only be solved by participants finding concrete answers in particular cases through an effort to accept the perspectives of all involved (p. 24). This departs from mere moral relativism, since Habermas feels that a universal principle assumes that all arguments deserve equal consideration regardless of their origin. It does, however, lead toward a state of indecisiveness, since one cannot fall back on rules and regulations but must work out what is right and proper within a network of communication. Therefore, Peter felt it important either for his analyst not be indifferent or for himself to have an internal dialogue that would hammer out the best course for him to pursue.

Seen in this way, that is, as a matter of argument and interpretation, neutrality becomes more like a launching point for deliberations. There is no solid and sure place for a resolution of certainty as one might hope would emerge from a repository of a set of laws. If there is no right answer, then it seems clear why a set of universal laws would have an appeal. However, it also seems reasonable to investigate how some individuals are very clear and decisive about right and wrong and how to behave; how some seem quite perplexed when confronted with gray areas of propriety; and how some seem not to concern themselves at all with these issues of correct and proper behavior. Psychoanalysis has traditionally turned to theories of superego development for its explanations of problems of morality and issues of moral guidance. That seems sufficient for some major questions involving right and wrong, but it may not suffice for many of the moral quandaries that occur in everyday life. A straightforward story involving identification with one's parents is surely an oversimplification. We turn next to an examination of the vicissitudes of developing a conscience and an unpacking of those words as well.

CHAPTER ELEVEN

Deontology and the Superego

Most psychoanalysts and psychotherapists are probably unfamiliar with the word *deontology*, which refers to one's obligations and personal imperatives, the language used to inform these, and their origin and development. Deontology is the study of duties or, according to some, the study of all of ethics. On the other hand, most analysts and therapists are quite familiar with the concept of the superego that they claim is the psychic repository of duties and ethical obligation. No claim can be made that these ideas are identical; yet the psychoanalytic study which is devoted to the development and status of the superego is often mistakenly understood as coterminous with the broader field of deontology and ethics in general.

The Superego

The forerunners of the superego are the experiences of parental prohibitions that the child learns to follow lest he or she lose the love of the parents. Fenichel said that these are essentially externalized "pre-superegos" which depend on a real and present external person for enforcement (1945, 103). The superego per se is formed later in development by the resolution of the Oedipus complex and the resulting identification with both parents. Freud described this process by noting that the forerunners combine with new introjects or identification, and together they form a modification or precipitate in the ego which stands apart from other ego constituents and is thus termed the superego or conscience.

Many problems result from the explanation offered by Freud, especially those that conclude that boys and girls combine features of both parents; in certain cultures, according to Fenichel, either the fatherly or the motherly superego seems dominant and therefore is culture specific. Another difficulty occurs in the effort to explain the relationship between the ego and the superego in the assignment of prohibitions to the one or to the other. For the most part, the experience of guilt is said to indicate superego injunctions.

Over time, a separate area of the superego has been identified as the ego ideal; the primary affect associated with problems in this psychic structure is shame (Piers and Singer 1953). A voluminous literature in psychoanalysis distinguishes between the circumstances that give rise to either guilt or shame, but we shall leave that to the side for the moment.

The explanations offered by Freud and classical psychoanalysis assume that a normative principle operates in superego and ego ideal formation. If someone has grown up in a reasonably functional family and has formed his or her identifications in a network of reciprocal expectations and perspectives, then it would follow that resulting moral judgments would be a standard for that person in that society. This leads to the idea of a healthy superego, and Freud in his paper on humor (1927) referred to a more positive role for one's conscience.

Beginning in 1969 and later elaborated, Lawrence Kohlberg (1984) proposed that moral judgments do exhibit the same structure in all cultures, because a series of invariant sequential stages proceed from the pre-superego forerunners of Freud to the final stage of rational moral thinking. His ideas followed the form of cognitive development that was formulated by Piaget (1932), and were an effort to universalize moral points of view. Such efforts are debated regularly in philosophical circles, and Kohlberg aimed to solve these debates by a scientific study of the psychological development of morality. Sadly, his stages are no longer taken seriously (Flanagan 1996, 132), but they do serve to highlight the effort to universalize and generalize moral theory, an effort pursued in different ways by psychology and philosophy.

Deontology

As noted earlier in this book, if we differentiate ethics from morality, we may say that ethics refer to what is good and the good life, while morality refers to what is both imperative and obligatory. Ethics is the aim at the good life, while morals are the adherence to laws or rules of behavior which may achieve that life. This division allows us to focus on the field of moral obligations or deontology while recognizing the primacy of the ethical over the moral. This also may allow us to focus on the psychological factors involved in moral issues. These factors are often employed to explain what composes the good life, a concept that is frequently but erroneously equated with deontology.

Many scholars have written extensively on the distinction between moral obligations and ethics or the proper way to live one's life. These writings more often than not are concerned with oppositions such as religion versus psychoanalysis, science versus humanism, or some variant of what is empirical and observable versus that which arises from faith or is said to be "universally true of all mankind." Paul Ricoeur, for example, explained Freud's failure to fully comprehend religion as related to his having no interest in the epigenesis of guilt. Ricoeur said this could have led him to better comprehend religion, but that his scientism prevented him from doing so (1970, 550). Flanagan says that one may maintain a scientific view of the world and yet make ample room for ethics by considering what he calls "ethics as human ecology" (2000, 265–320). He dislikes the idea of putting ethics on one side and science on the other because, for him, doing science at all involves a host of normative commitments (Flanagan 1996, 122). His solution is to seek a link between science, which he says is universal, and ethics, which is local and variable. Of course, this sounds like another distinction between morals or local laws and ethics as the good life for all mankind, that is, the manner in which one should live.

In contrast with Flanagan, W. V. Quine feels that science is distinct from ethics in that science has goals such as truth and prediction, while ethics is "methodologically infirm"; its goals are vague unless one posits getting into heaven as a goal (1969, 69–90).

There is, as noted above, a continuing set of oppositional ideas that ring through many of these discussions, ranging from ethics versus morals, to science versus humanism, to local versus universal, to vagueness versus definitiveness, et cetera, et cetera. In an original perspective on this subject, B. Litowitz (2004) distinguishes between deontic and epistemic communication and so deepens the discussion of the way in which language contributes to the understanding of the development of moral judgment. *Deontic* refers to morals and permissions, while *epistemic* refers to judgment.

Litowitz notes that most psychoanalytic scholars view ethics as based on prepositional language, and thereby it is assumed to be relevant to the oedipal period and its resolution. This is based on superego formation after age three. Her contrary view is that the adult-infant dyad is social from birth, and that deontological issues involving obligations, permissions, and responsibilities emerge from and define these earliest pre-oedipal relationships. She further states that there are continuing ambiguities and uncertainties involving these connections, and that this is what is most noteworthy in all of our patients—the lack of certainty in moral dilemmas.

Perhaps the most striking part of the Litowitz thesis is that the accompanying affect to this state of ambiguity is that of shame rather than guilt. One way of putting this all together would be to see the forerunners of the superego as requiring the love and approval of the parents, who are needed as an external presence in order to validate the child's actions. Loss of this approval or validation leads to the painful affect of shame. There remains a lack of clarity in the gestural or nonlinguistic nature of this form of message exchange, resulting in an inherent ambiguity in these interactions. As the superego is more firmly established, guilt becomes dominant. Next this new internalized structure is intertwined with its forerunners, but prior to this development it is regulated by the dominant feeling of guilt or anticipated punishment. As language becomes more prepositional, certainty becomes more likely.

It is always difficult to disentangle complex affect states, although now we are able to consider shame as having an earlier origin than guilt (Tomkins 1962–63). A self-psychological view posits that an act of the self that is a derivative of a grandiose, exhibitionistic display requires a mirroring or validating response from a self object. If this fails to occur, there is a flooding of the self with shameful and embarrassing affect. Thus, for example, one might feel humiliated when caught in an act of seeming greedy or of cheating. One might postulate an experience of guilt only if some punitive action were to ensue as a result of this supposed greed. If one also had an idealizing relationship with the observing other, then one could also postulate that a failure to live up to his or her ideals might also usher in a shameful episode. This is illustrated in the case of Peter in chapter 10.

Although Litowitz differentiates deontic from epistemic modes of speaking and proceeds to distinguish the first, which arrives as earlier and ambiguous, from the second, which arrives later and deals with the real state of the world, it is debatable whether and when we are able to be safely sure about anything. If we imagine a continuum of moral standards, we can place some moral struggles at a point of certain prohibitions followed by guilt, one example of which might be murder. We can then proceed to find other prohibitions that involve a mixture of shame and guilt, such as might occur in sexual aberrations. Along this continuum we become less certain and less clear about the accompanying affect, as we saw earlier in the situation of Peter and the free drugs.

If a further modification is introduced to the classical theory of oedipal resolution, then we may succeed at a tighter explanation of the stages of superego formation. Self psychology takes the position that the oedipal phase can only be understood when it is viewed within the context of the child's emotional milieu (Ornstein and Ornstein 2005, 239). A conflict-ridden Oedipus results from failures of caregivers to properly respond to the child's competitive behavior. Therefore, one may experience either a normal or nonpathological oedipal phase or one that is characterized by self-object failures both before and during this developmental phase. Thus, a problematic or pathological superego must, by definition, contain both the forerunners and its own deficits from moments of parental failure. This view contrasts sharply with that of Arlow, who thought that emphasizing traumatic experiences or relationships in the first or second year of life is unwise, because they occur during a period when the child has only needs and no responsibilities and hence no need to feel guilty (1991, 13). Arlow's position makes no allowance for pre-oedipal shame and is directly contradicted by the position articulated above by Litowitz as well as by the work of Izard (1971) and Tomkins (1962–63), who extensively studied shame as a fundamental affect. As noted, shame operates after some action that involves a need for a confirming reaction. It underlies a number of feelings such as inferiority, shyness, guilt, and discouragement. Thus, because shame is a core affect, we are unable to always sharply distinguish it from guilt, especially as one deals with moral transgressions. Nor can we generalize about the assumption that superego development inevitably results in affects of guilt for all forms of moral problems. It seems more likely that the added ingredient of parental anger and possible punishment causes the experience of guilt. Some moral transgressions lead primarily to shame, some to an admixture of shame and guilt, and some primarily to guilt. We might postulate that an ideal or perhaps fictitious psyche could be possessed of moral standards with no accompanying negative affective experiences of either shame or guilt.

Rational Moral Judgments

One would hope that an inner or private and personal debate about the pros and cons of a moral dilemma would ultimately yield a rational decision. If this would prove to be unsuccessful or unlikely, then an argument with another person with another point of view might result in an outcome or decision based on reason. If these two persons would agree to be open and honest, refrain from coercion, and allow for equal participation, then surely over time a consensus would be reached and some degree of certainty attained. This kind of discourse moves away from a single person involved in an effort to follow the logic of reaching personal moral grounding to an exchange of ideas in which self-reflection necessarily gives way to a perspective that goes beyond the individual. Of course, there is no guarantee that there is a correct answer to every question. To emphasize the rational means only to make an effort to reduce or eliminate the irrational. Psychoanalysis would concern itself with the recognition of irrational unconscious elements in order to free the decision maker from these contaminating contributions.

Once liberated from the remnants of childhood and unconscious fantasies about propriety and punishment, rational judgment becomes more possible. This is not to say that there are no participating strong emotions in one's decision, since the resolution is certainly not all cognitive. However, there are accompanying emotions of satisfaction and pride in reaching a point of correctness. They are not driven by anxiety. Moreover, there is a goal that is implicit in this search for the rational, and it is the goal of clarity. Failure to reach this end point is a call for assistance, and this is often the occasion for an exchange of ideas which can achieve this goal.

Analysts and therapists may well begin their work by allowing the patient to make one or another moral judgment with no interference from the analyst save that of the above-noted removing of obstacles. What may result from this rather single-minded effort is often less than satisfactory, since the very foundations of morality are rooted in ambiguity and uncertainty. Vagueness seems to haunt this effort. If one struggles with a decision about whether to carry an umbrella, the state of the world will let you know if your decision, your judgment, was correct. Not so with moral judgments, since only your state of mind guides your sense of conviction. Whereas most judgments can answer to the world, moral judgments seem more social or seem to seek an answer from one person to another.

When a patient enlists his therapist or analyst in resolving a dilemma, there seems to be a better chance that the dialogue will yield a more optimal result than would occur in solitary self-reflection. The consideration of a conversation opens up an entirely new dimension: we recognize that two people in conversation, while they should ideally try to understand each other, are using words that may carry different meanings to each speaker. The yield of such conversations should enable each person not only to understand the other's point of view but also to better understand his own. Our language, especially about morals and values, is said to be contingent, or, as Webster says, apt to be affected by unforeseen circumstances, unfixed, or dependent on something else. We change our minds as we talk about things, not only because we hear another point of view but also because we hear ourselves. What may result is less a grounding in certainty than something closer to a groundless belief (M. Williams 1999).

Here is an example of a dilemma that would seem to be readily resolvable but defied a neat solution. There was no clear rule, and it seemed to be a matter of opinion.

Case Illustration

At the termination of her therapy, Mrs. A. announced to her psychotherapist that she wished to give him a gift of several thousand dollars above and beyond her usual payments. She could well afford such a gift, and she was extremely grateful to her therapist for what had been achieved. The therapist was initially pleased and surprised, but he lost no time in informing his patient that he by no means could accept such a gift. As a compromise, he suggested that the patient consider making a charitable contribution, and after some soul-searching offered his psychiatric hospital as a possible worthwhile recipient.

Privately, Mrs. A.'s therapist felt that his treatment of his patient had not been sufficiently intense, inasmuch as his patient did not feel fully emancipated from the transference, as evidenced by her persistent feeling of indebtedness. He decided not to pursue a resolution of this impasse, and so terminated the treatment. Shortly thereafter he learned of the finalization of the previously announced donation.

In sharp contrast with the experience of Mrs. A. and her therapist, Dr. S. had a somewhat similar experience with a strikingly different ending. He had completed what he thought to be a well-conducted analysis with a reasonably successful termination. Some years later he learned of the death of his patient, and one day was startled to hear from a lawyer that he had been given a bequest in the patient's will. Dr. S. could not explain this gift as a result of an incompletely resolved transference, nor was he in any position to contemplate that possibility. Whereas one could readily see how the offer or presentation of a gift during an analysis would be an object of inquiry, including the possibility of the relevance of the analyst's desire, there was no question of this as far as Dr. S. was concerned. Rather, he likened it to hearing of a bequest from a long-forgotten relative. However, he hesitated to leave it at that and asked for opinions from several colleagues. There was no consensus, and no one ever found out if he took the money.

The first therapist felt that he could not take the offered money from Mrs. A. with a clear conscience. The moral failing that he felt followed from his conviction that a well-treated patient would not continue to feel indebted to her therapist, and so he could not take advantage of this situation. Furthermore, he was convinced that it was never proper to take gifts from patients, inasmuch as the rules of psychiatry made it clear that the fee was all the psychiatrist could ask from a patient. Mrs. A.'s therapist may have indeed been scornful of Dr. S.

Dr. S. had no pangs of guilt whatsoever about being named in his patient's will, and if asked, would have said that this case was not at all identical to that of Mrs. A. and her therapist. The gratitude of his now deceased patient was only that and nothing more. One could certainly posit some remnant of unanalyzed material that was connected to this act of appreciation, but surely all analyses leave something untouched. Dr. S. felt he had a clear conscience, especially since discussions with his colleagues were of little help; no one could come up with a rule that applied to this situation.

When one person understands another by way of empathy, there may result a range of opinions, in contrast with an appraisal determined by an unchallenged set of objective facts. A given sentence spoken by different persons or by the same person at different times usually does not mean the same thing. One cannot objectively determine what a sentence stands for without an effort to first understand the speaker. If we add another ingredient to this equation—that of the listener's own personal assessment of what he or she hears—then we have embarked on the investigation of the dialogue. Interpretation of the written or spoken word involves the meaning that emerges from the completed circle of the listener grasping the total content of the speaker, modified by whatever particular preconception that listener brings to the encounter.

Rational judgment is not decisive, because there is no final court of appeal. To paraphrase what M. Williams (1999) has concluded: Human knowledge is an evolving social phenomenon. We have a core of unquestioned ideas against which more marginal and less certain beliefs can be checked. But even this core may be drastically revised as the result of deeper insight or theoretical advance. Any belief can be questioned, but not all at once. The pursuit of knowledge as well as of moral values is a rational pursuit not because it rests on a foundation but because it is a self-correcting enterprise.

Back to Deontology

It is a difficult decision to embrace the idea of moral relativism, because this position can be seen as reflecting an "anything goes" philosophy that promotes moral laxity or immorality. It is also difficult to accept a fixed set of moral standards, because they may be accompanied by strict and unyielding guidelines for behavior that can be regulated by threats and punitive actions. One suggested alternative to this impossible choice is one that is often confused with relativism, namely subjectivism, or the making of decisions based on personal preferences or opinions.

We are now able to recognize that any given event or situation is open to multiple interpretations, and this recognition may serve to unite these three options. We may be able to combine moral guidelines and personal prejudices with a modicum of lasting uncertainty. In such a pursuit we also realize that each and every decision causes us to remake ourselves. Our capacity to do so may be limited, and it is a never-finished task. This remaking is offered as a way of conceptualizing psychotherapy and psychoanalysis. The mutual interaction of analyst and patient is a series of negotiations based on our own individual histories. We also engage a particular scientific enterprise that limits our range of influence. While some therapists and analysts may yearn for a set of moral guidelines, the greater likelihood is that we work best in an atmosphere of uncertainty.

What we have learned from the development of our individual consciences and the set of moral imperatives that serve whatever community in which we live is once again the virtue of pragmatism. If indeed we do not prejudge situations but consider each anew, then we might make a claim for a neutral position as an ideal pragmatic starting point. Unfortunately, that, too, can lead to difficulties, inasmuch as one man's neutrality need not match that of another. We do not seem possessed of an internal barometer for right and wrong, but rather of a need for an exchange of ideas and opinions to make a moral determination. The idea of a rather stable superego is probably an unlikely comfort.

CHAPTER TWELVE

Choosing Up Sides

The Problem

In answering a question about his personal struggle with moral issues, one analyst with a wide range of experience said that his entire life of practice had had to do with moral quandaries of one form or another. The same question put to another psychoanalyst of equal seniority and sincerity was answered with the somewhat casual comment that such issues were not of much moment at all. The second felt his practice was devoted to the faithful application of a technique, one that he felt he had mastered fairly well. It did not consist of offering opinions, or of telling people how to live; that was not his job. The first responder was convinced that, like it or not, it had become his job. How could this be, that two analysts had such disparate ideas about their life's work? One possibility was that the question was vague; it could be that moral issues and dilemmas and quandaries simply meant different things to different people. Should that be?

The first person, who told of endless struggles in his professional life, immediately related a representative list ranging from changing codes on insurance claims in order to benefit his patients, to seeing people who had histories of criminal behavior, to wanting to tell a naïve patient that his or her spouse was surely unfaithful, and on and on. The second, more sanguine, person said that he could indeed recall one occasion when he had published a case report without asking permission of the patient, but that was long ago, when permission was not considered necessary. Since then he had not published at all. Ergo, no quandaries. When pressed further with the above list of his anonymous colleague, he said in a rather conspiratorial voice that he felt that his entire life, both inside and outside of his practice, was a moral dilemma which he chose to deny. Thereby he was able, by dint of denial, to claim a certain calm about those issues that plagued others. Indeed, he felt that he was a moral person, one who behaved properly and correctly with his patients, one who had never faced an ethics board, and one who could be rather strict and even punitive with those who were found participating in moral transgressions.

Our more troubled analyst experienced no such serenity. He was never sure of the propriety of his conduct. He had been chastised more than once by colleagues in his clinical case presentations, was extremely tolerant and forgiving of others who had been found to be less than honorable, and envied anyone who was comfortable and secure in his dealings with such problematic arenas.

Perhaps most mental health professionals might say that they live in the space between these two positions. If one is equipped with a set of clear moral guidelines, there may be struggles that qualify as dilemmas. That is, if one is fortunate enough to rarely, if ever, encounter such uncertainties, then the question of how one behaves honorably simply does not arise. However, the lack of such a struggle may be a clue to the feature that is missing in some treatment situations, although it may dominate others. The following is an example.

Case Illustration

Ken was a convicted felon of white-collar crimes who had entered psychotherapy as part of a plea bargain arranged at his sentencing. After some time in treatment, he managed to persevere in the straight and narrow, with no evidence of immoral or illegal behavior. His work often took him out of town, but he usually managed to keep his psychotherapy appointments, inasmuch as he felt them to be the key factor in his new life of honesty and integrity. He had become a good patient.

One day Ken phoned his psychiatrist-therapist from a distant city to say that his flight had been cancelled, but that he had managed to get a seat on another flight by claiming that he had to keep an urgent appointment with his doctor. He had used his psychiatrist's name, so he wanted to alert him about a possible call to confirm what was essentially a lie, since Ken had no appointment for several days.

When this vignette was presented to a group of analysts and therapists, they all agreed that the patient was trying to have his therapist collude with him in his dishonesty. The discussion that followed had to do with the variety of ways that this therapist might or perhaps ought to respond. All agreed that this patient should not get away with his lie.

When I suggested in an earlier chapter a list of moral positions that psychoanalysts are asked to adopt, it was noted that some items on the list were easy to agree with, while others were more difficult to achieve. Honesty, for one, was easy to include, in contrast with problems associated with (say) clinical case publication. Thus, when Ken's therapist was asked by the group about his response to his patient, the therapist felt it very important to emphasize that he himself had a personal dislike of airline regulations and certainly would have wanted to do just what Ken had done. In his response to Ken he had laughed, but he was also able to feel exactly as Ken had felt as well as to know how others might feel. The therapist's position that he spelled out to the group was that his capacity to be dishonest was something that had enabled him over time to both understand and help Ken.

The list of qualities demanded of a therapist is never revised to include the requirement of dishonesty along with honesty. The same might be said of all the other virtues that fail to encompass the full range of complex configurations that enable us to understand others. Ken's therapist felt that a total embrace of honesty as a personal requirement would effectively foreclose the possibility of helping his patient. How could one understand dishonesty unless one had lived it? This, of course, leads to the larger question of how anyone can understand another if the experience of that other is alien or objectionable. We seem able to be empathic with someone of another gender because we do share both masculine and feminine traits. We may struggle with comprehending someone from a completely foreign culture, and much of a successful outcome in that regard depends on finding some commonality of experience. However, when we approach an issue that we find objectionable and/or immoral, we are often at an impasse in achieving an empathic connection, and we tend to fall back on attitudes of righteousness and condemnation, just as did our friend from Philadelphia in chapter 7. More often than not, we have managed to disavow that unacceptable feeling, and we need to reconnect with it in order to easily understand some position. In fact, we are routinely unable to comprehend certain actions of others until and unless we gain access to similar feelings harbored within us.

Our confident analyst described earlier may have chosen to inform Ken that he could not support the effort of this or any patient to enlist him in a project that was in any way outside of normal rules and regulations. In this manner, he may have been able to communicate to Ken that he himself was incorruptible as well as to demonstrate to Ken how morally correct people behaved. One may correctly surmise that Ken surely knew all of this, and that this admonition was mainly for the analyst's benefit. Most efforts to point out one's moral probity to others are not made in order to provide information, yet they are rarely concealed because they are satisfying for the sermonizer.

Our more conflicted analyst may have chosen to support Ken in this act of deception and may even have shared his own proclivities in this direction. That he may have been troubled about this is not in question, since he has always been candid about this difficulty in similar areas of conflict about right and wrong. One might surmise that Ken would not be surprised at this sharing of dishonesty, and it might even be imagined that Ken had done what he did in order to test his therapist. Sharing how one feels is championed by some therapists (Bridges 2005, 8) as one guide to the proper conduct of therapy. However, most efforts to disclose our feelings to our patients should be carefully scrutinized for the possibility of their being self-serving. The patient may be better served by feelings being concealed, since revelation tends to derail the conversation.

Ken's own therapist could neither scold nor support his patient, since he was able to see both the moral and the immoral as operating simultaneously in Ken's situation. One may argue at this point that the crucial issue is the person's proper conduct rather than what one may or may not be thinking or feeling. Thus, the private thoughts of the therapist should possibly be contained while the proper message is delivered. However, this points out the problem that writers who encourage openness and sharing along with those who urge prompt condemnation of delinquency routinely overlook: what is the ultimate impact of such openness?

Nonetheless, a correct therapeutic interpretation is called for here, and it points to the folly of pursuing the path of revealing one's feelings to the patient, either those of agreement or those of condemnation. The therapist who is able to experience his or her own duality is equipped to interpret the same split or duality in the patient (Goldberg 2002). This interpretation recognizes that Ken knows both what is correct and what is not so. What he does not know is the origin and coexistence of this split. That should be the work of psychotherapy.

People in moral dilemmas often have splits similar to persons like Ken who struggle over doing what society feels is the right thing. Our previously characterized conscientious analyst was aware of his personal sense of struggle, but his virtuous self clearly outweighed the potentially delinquent one. Our discontented analyst had no such state of comfort, because the odds for him were not in favor of moral certitude. His was a constant battle, because his split or duality was too evenhanded or perhaps too balanced to offer him the hope of a peaceful resolution. Ken was initially quite the opposite of our secure analyst, but over time he became a man in constant and persistent struggle over opting for virtue versus misbehavior.

It would appear from the above that the argument about self-disclosure is a nonargument, inasmuch as at times it may be helpful and, at times, harmful (Gutheil and Gabbard 1993, 412). It may allow for self-reflection on either the patient's or the therapist's part; however, it is not to be equated or confused with interpretation, which it may serve to obviate. This is especially true in situations where the therapist disavows the segment of his personality that is similar to that of the patient's. By saying how one feels, one may miss the chance to recognize how one may rather not feel.

Virtue Disavowed

Once the therapist is equipped with insight into the duality of his or hers that corresponds to the split in the patient, the opportunity for an effective interpretation is available. Indeed, it is probably true that one can appreciate and strive to solve moral dilemmas only if both sides of the situation can be properly—ideally, simultaneously—experienced. Interestingly, this duality of experience is equally true of patients, some of whom are not in touch with the morally correct behaving segment because it tends to be disavowed as one pursues delinquency or misbehavior. Thus, Ken's therapist needed to help Ken to see that *he also* wanted to tell the truth. It should go without saying that this is not to be communicated as a moral lesson, but rather as a recognition that Ken can be torn between disparate aspects of himself. This vision of countertransference is not one usually entertained, but it is offered here as paradigmatic for moral and/or ethical dilemmas. It harkens back to what was previously noted with regard to deontology and the origins of our moral tenets. The amalgamation of components of the superego and ego ideal does not lend itself to a convenient set of standards for proper behavior, but rather encompasses a range of responses which may reside at opposing poles of permissive behavior and misbehavior. Ambiguity is often the norm.

If one is able to see both sides of a dilemma, the capacity to make an informed decision is heightened. Too often we engage in automatic responses of righteousness, and by doing so we foreclose what may be different responses from those in a debate in which one side is chosen over another. If Ken can gain insight into the fact that he wants to lie as well as to be honest, then the current problem may open an inquiry into the origin of his duality and lead to a better understanding of his daily psychology, which often has to mediate between these parallel selves.

As it turns out, Ken's childhood was one of alternate and opposing sets of strictness and indulgence, and his adult personality maintained this split psychological structure. His treatment needed to be aimed at integration and not at the dominance of one sector, for instance the morally correct one, over another. Only a therapist who is able to adequately experience these parallel selves is able in turn to afford Ken the therapeutic activity that is required, while any form of instruction or permission becomes a product of the therapist's persuasion.

When Ken's parents were divorced and he went to live with his mother, he was able to be with his father only under a set of conditions imposed by his mother. These conditions consisted of his never revealing any sign of either wanting to be with his father or enjoying the time spent with his father. Rather, he was required to look unhappy after a visit and to show reluctance at the time of an anticipated visit. He was forced to live a lie.

Ken's father was a fun-loving, hard-drinking, nonconforming man in vivid contrast with his mother, who was sober, depressed, and a model of propriety. Ken felt sorry for his mother while longing to spend more time with his father. While initially Ken's treatment had much to do with behavior that seemed characteristic of his now-deceased dad, after some time Ken was more in touch with his identification with his mother, and so with his positive experience of honesty but also of depression. It seemed likely that his disavowal of this sector of his personality was protective of this depressive state that dominated his life as well.

If Ken were to revisit the moment that he chose to lie in order to get a seat on a flight versus tell the truth and have his flight delayed, he would then be in the grips of a true moral dilemma: one which represented two sides with equal rights to be heard and responded to. Whereas previously Ken allowed only the single voice of doing what was necessary to get his way, now he was able to experience and examine the vivid opposition that should be the core of a true dilemma.

It is by definition extremely unlikely that one ever meets a dishonest person who does not also know what it is to be honest. It is therefore of no value whatsoever to consider a presentation of information called for to address dishonesty. Aside from certain pathological conditions such as *pseudologica fantastica*, wherein it is said that lying is compulsive and unregulated, most acts of dishonesty are directed toward achieving certain goals with a minimum of discomfort. Complications may occur when one is uncertain as to whether it is honesty or dishonesty that will achieve the desired goal. This is one form of a dilemma, that is, the question of what indeed is the best policy or what will work best. Moral dilemmas do not pose this problem, but rather raise another sort of question that asks what one can live with in terms of guilt or shame. However, in order to achieve self-awareness of this form of dilemma, equal weight must be given to each side of the equation.

Achieving a Balance

If we generalize beyond the virtue of honesty, we are able to see that it is not merely a question of opting for one side over another on the basis of goals or of doing what is intellectually acceptable. Rather, it has much to do with the polar sets of feelings and identifications with which one lives. People who cheat a little on their income tax do so because they can get away with it and likely not feel guilty at doing so. The decision about such cheating is routinely a conscious one, much like any debate over possible courses of action that offer fairly equal resulting satisfactions. This is not the case for moral decisions that are based on absolute or unquestioned positions which do not allow a disavowed element to have a say.

Psychoanalysts and psychotherapists have a distinctly different role to play than that of ethicists or moralists in distinguishing *why* someone does something rather than *if* someone should do something. When it comes to the rules and regulations of their own professional practice, however, they should examine *why* they feel compelled to follow one form of conduct rather than another as well as *if* they should do so. Thus, when it is taken as gospel that everything the patient reports is confidential, we need to scrutinize both the origin and the wisdom of that injunction. This need not result in a change of such guidance, but it may well result in a better understanding of our patients.

The range of indiscretions that confront some therapists often exceeds that found in normal relationships. Some potential discretions are unique, some repressed, and some disavowed. One analyst reported that he could not attend a patient's art show because his training insisted that all contact between patient and analyst be restricted to the analytic hours. This hardly ranks as a moral issue, no matter how much one may agree or disagree with it. Another analyst declared himself unable to treat a pedophile because he felt the activity to be so repugnant that he could never be empathic with this perverse patient. One might here hazard a guess as to his own pedophilic impulses being repressed, but probably this line of inquiry would never advance much beyond conjecture. A more striking example of disavowal is that of the analyst who began a sexual affair with his patient with the rationalization that it was to be an affair that had nothing whatsoever to do with her treatment. That analyst was well able to "know" that what he was doing was against the rules and regulations of his profession, but only after years of treatment following this unfortunate occurrence was he able to ask himself what in the world he had been thinking. Not surprisingly, his treatment was conducted by an analyst who could well imagine engaging in such a forbidden behavior, but felt himself incapable of doing so. He could think of it but not do it.

It was both interesting and fascinating to observe the slow encroachment of the disavowed material into an integrated state in the analyst-patient. Initially, the sexual activity was easily condoned and rationalized along with total recognition of what others might say and think. Over time this essentially unfelt—that is, known about but not experienced—conflict was able to be felt, and there ensued an alteration, with one side winning dominance over the other. Thus, for this patient, there was a true dilemma as to right and wrong. The accompanying shame over his indiscretion allowed for a resolution of the dilemma. Indeed, the relative weight of the associated affects seems to be the crucial determinant for dilemma resolution.

Moral Blindness

In contrast with these analysts who admitted to personal moral dilemmas, some analysts claim none, either in themselves or in their patients. While we may be on safe ground with the tentative assumption that such a position is unlikely, there should be no doubt that it demands another sort of explanation. We can arrive at this explanation by determining if the vertical split of any given patient is able to be matched by a complementary split in the analyst. Just as some analysts work better with some patients than with others, it seems without question that some analysts will be incapable of allowing such a split transference to develop and be recognized. Rather than attribute this sort of failing to a deficiency or resistance in the analyst, it may well be the case that his or her own psychic organization does not allow for this complementary state. One can imagine all sorts of reasons for this incapacity, ranging from a too firm sense of self to a self on the verge of fragmentation, but it is sufficient to recognize it as a valid limitation for some therapists and analysts. This limitation is equivalent to a form of blindness in the sense that any obstacle to an empathic position toward or understanding of another person denotes an incapacity to see what needs to be seen. This should not, however, be taken as an indictment against the therapist, but rather as a signal and a reminder that attributing necessary and/or essential characteristics to a therapist (Buechler 2004) is an act of folly, since there can never be a set of universal characteristics for either therapists or patients.

Lacking a capacity to see both sides of an issue, no matter how abhorrently one may feel about what one is asked to experience, is an absolute impediment to the resolution of a dilemma. One cannot pick one side over the other until both sides are represented. The inevitable result of such moral blindness is a wholesale embrace of what can be readily seen, along with a dismissal of the nonrepresented parallel self. This is the proper position that we often attribute to ethics boards, which need not take into account the legitimacy of a vertical split or the origins of a disavowed sector. Such boards are not assigned the task of determining why the offender did what he or she did, but occasionally this becomes a factor in adjudicating what is felt to be a proper remedy and/or punishment. In a similar manner, therapists who should primarily be curious as to why the person did what was done often become carried away by ethical or moral considerations. It is to be hoped that a better appreciation of the nature of moral dilemmas can bring some clarity to the ethical therapeutic muddle.

CHAPTER THIRTEEN

Making Morals Manifest

There is no clear and uncomplicated way to describe what is required of psychoanalysts and psychotherapists in terms of personal characterization. Some of today's psychiatrists are biologically biased and not much interested in therapy, and some openly confess that they have no wish to become emotionally involved with their patients. When writers such as Buechler (2004, 2) say that treatment is inherently a life-and-death struggle that takes enormous commitment and energy, they present what some may say is an extreme position, and in so doing they might well frighten the fledgling therapist. When analysts such as Searles (1965) caution us against too much therapeutic zeal, they may well lend some comfort to someone who fears that too much may be demanded in undertaking such a task as psychotherapy. However, when Lander (2003) writes that the analyst occupies a place of listening without exercising value judgments, he seems quite at odds with an interpersonal analyst who writes that interpersonal psychoanalysis is pragmatic, flexible, and down-to-earth because it deals with what actually transpires between people and how they live (and structure) that experience (Lionells et al. 1995, 4). It seems both legitimate and prudent to look for a place for oneself between cool detachment and that aforementioned life-and-death struggle. As a matter of fact, that search for a position or place can be considered essentially as much a moral decision as a scientific one. What is best for a patient should ideally be a product of scientific scrutiny, but, lacking that source of certainty, it routinely becomes a matter of opinion. These opinions are necessarily subjective and open to debate and discussion, which, unfortunately, lead to camps of opposition rather than to consensus and resolution.

Opposing sets of ideas and differing theories of operation are really not the problem, and they should not be seen as illustrative of some sort of evidence that psychotherapy and psychoanalysis are inexact sciences. Rather, these oppositions may not be relevant to psychotherapy per se. We all know or should know that many patients seem to improve with any one of a wide spectrum of therapists, and there are as yet no definitive conclusions as to what is best for one person rather than another in terms of either the personality of the therapist or his/her operating theory. Well-intentioned therapists do champion the method of practice that they pursue, and they often come to believe and to insist on theirs being proper and correct while considering others misguided, ill-informed, or at times even harmful. While one psychotherapist urges a mutual feeling of love for successful therapy, another insists that there is no place in treatment for personal values; while one urges self-disclosure, another finds virtue only in anonymity. It is incumbent on us to begin to investigate why these irreconcilable differences exist. Such an initial investigation may better succeed in determining the meaning of these convictions, rather than which position deserves the crown of competence.

When we say that the determining factors in choosing one form of therapy over another or of valuing one set of personality traits of therapists over another are basically moral issues, we are saying no more than that we are guided by certain rules and regulations that we deem correct and proper rather than merely expedient for what we do. When we further claim that these moral factors are often not readily apparent or, at times, even able to be articulated, we aim to highlight their existence as well as to make clear that they are best seen as beliefs and opinions that often may fail the test of scientific scrutiny. Therefore, it may well be true that some therapists who profess love for patients do indeed serve them well, while others who champion anonymity are equally successful. Probably neither would recognize their stances as being members of a moral order, nor would they agree to this characterization. When pushed, they may defend what they do on the basis of its being proper, correct, and called for. Like it or not, that is what moral principles are all about.

Nonspecific Factors

In 1961, Jerome Frank wrote a book titled *Persuasion and Healing* that stressed the ubiquitousness of the "non-specific factors" in all forms of psychotherapy. The text emphasized the therapist's faith in the efficacy of his or her efforts, and that particular dimension has been carried forth today in the studies on suggestion and the placebo effect. These factors are nonspecific in that they apply to any and all efforts involving therapy, and they might even be illustrated by the experiment mentioned in chapter 3, in which patients were fooled into speaking to a nonexistent therapist. The improvement that may have resulted from this encounter cannot possibly be attributed to anything other than some belief or hope or expectation that is engendered in the patient. This is one form of a placebo in that nothing that is considered active or capable of affecting a change is administered to an unwitting patient. Frank added to what would be a purely neutral effect expected of a placebo by his recognition of the overt or covert communication by the therapist to the patient that he or she believed in the potential of this other particular perspective on cure. Hope and faith became central factors. All sorts of conclusions can be reached as to this being sufficient for some and meaningless for others, but it may be thought of as a baseline for therapy in general. We all start with a leg up by engendering hope and faith. What follows may or may not be of help, but it must be specifically added to the nonspecific factors.

Specific Factors

If we add the specific form of intervention that is highlighted by way of the diverse forms of psychoanalysis and psychotherapy, we can only then begin to hope to see how one form of treatment may be better than another. Thus, psychoanalysis can claim that making the unconscious conscious is the crucial ingredient that differentiates it from other therapeutic interventions, and so that activity also is the necessary factor for patient improvement. Of course, this is not the place to delineate the distinguishing components of the varieties of therapy, but it is worthwhile to separate whatever is felt to be central and significant from what is ancillary and yet important. For example, a psychoanalyst may say that making conscious the unconscious is central, while certainly agreeing that confidentiality, as prized as it is, is not essential to the cure of the patient. It (confidentiality) is important, but alone it is hardly the vehicle of improvement. At times some varieties of therapy seem to falter at this suggested division of labor, and we read the literature on self-disclosure, for instance, which is claimed to benefit both therapist and patient (Maroda 1999b). That appears to move the focus from factors that were long considered enabling to a position of central efficacy. A perhaps poor analogy serves to illustrate the point: the surgeon who scrubs his hands separates that ancillary action from the surgery proper. No such clarity is attributable to many forms of psychotherapy, although this attribution of vagueness is sometimes itself considered a crucial component of cure, as when Maroda writes: "It seems that once we admitted to our countertransference and the mutuality of the therapeutic relationship, we did not have a clear idea of how it should be handled" (1999a, 101–2). The state of uncertainty that is said to preface self-disclosure is carried by one writer to a plea for a space for "playful creativity" (Buechler 2004, 175), and there can be little doubt that for some this state has moved to a central position of necessity in the psychotherapeutic process.

Vagueness Made Manifest

A poignant story of self-disclosure is told by one analyst, who uses a clinical vignette to underscore the need for a patient to experience a new relationship with the analyst as part of a developmental experience (Shane, Shane, and Gales 1997, 149). Here, an activity that is sometimes equated with either a virtuous action that enables a therapist to feel "less lonely" or even a "self-revealing venture in a spirit of repentance, in the sense of making up for the sins of our analytic fathers" (Buechler 2004, 174) is transformed into a specific technical tool. Of course, it is open to argument whether treatment is tantamount to a new developmental opportunity, but it at least is open. Nor could one possibly dispute the value of any therapist doing something about his or her loneliness. The difference is striking: either there is a specific reason for doing or not doing something directed toward patient improvement, or there is a general suggestion for being something or someone that facilitates treatment. A third possibility exists: that much of what is done or recommended has little or nothing to do with patient improvement. Rather, it is a part of custom or tradition that persists and is handed down as some form of historical necessity.

All three of the ways of being a therapist and doing therapy inevitably become wrapped in the mantle of correctness and are promulgated as moral necessities. If a recommendation is made for a relational approach to psychotherapy, it is often accompanied by a parallel suggestion that therapists will experience personal growth and satisfaction and even "access new strands of their own life narratives" (Frawley-O'Dea and Sarnat 2001, 69). Whereas this may be seen as a byproduct of practicing psychotherapy, it runs the risk of becoming a measuring rod of success. It is clearly not the same as asking that one's countertransference be analyzed so as not to offer impediments to the treatment. A case can be made that an effective treatment should leave the therapist unscathed. This ambiguity is not likely to be resolved without attention being paid to the moral and ethical issues involved.

The rather regular recommendations that psychoanalysis and psycho-therapy become subjected to empirical studies as to their efficacy and so compared with nonpsychological interventions may be doomed to failure, not because of the complexity of the subjects or the indifference of their practitioners, but rather because so much of what is done has to do with implicit moral activity that remains unacknowledged and unexamined.

Midst the nonspecific factors such as hope and the specific ones such as interpreting the unconscious lie a host of implicit assumptions that are said to be either critical or indispensable to an analyst or a therapist. That quality of necessity leads to their failing to be made explicit and/or to be challenged. At some point they become raised to the status of virtues, and are thereupon immune to further examination.

Only when our implicit suppositions are made explicit can they be empirically studied and compared. Only when all the moral virtues that are routinely called for and defended are tested in some sort of theoretical crucible can they be taken as gospel. At this point in time, we have no reason aside from special pleading, defined as an argument that ignores all unfavorable evidence, to insist on therapists being kind or courageous or honest any more than they should be mean, cowardly, and untruthful. Nor can we possibly elevate confidentiality to an absolute place in treatment, let alone assume that all patients will emerge as considerate and thoughtful people. Indeed, our assumptions can be as much an obstacle as a guide. To ask that we become explicit about our moral standards is not to suggest that we abandon them. Quite the opposite: it lends them a possible foundation, albeit a foundation that lacks permanence. My earlier plea for moral ambiguity is best seen as a possible first step toward moral certainty, which, we now recognize, is only approached, never achieved.

In his personal reflections on the question of right and wrong, theologian Harvey Cox confessed that our best-informed decisions may be wrong, and he quoted Oliver Cromwell as saying, "I beseech you in the bowels of Christ, think it possible you may be mistaken" (Cox 2004, 296). Cox felt that the best he could hope for in teaching his students about moral choices was that they come to the realization that others might arrive at decisions quite different from their own, along with the realization that they themselves may have been mistaken. Yet that knowledge need not carry over into changing one's mind or modifying what Cox called moral courage, the fortitude to remain steadfast in one's decision.

I think a psychoanalyst would wonder about the unconscious components that allowed one either to remain convinced in spite of contrary arguments or to somehow know right from wrong without good reason. So many of Cox's students insisted that they knew what was right, but they could not defend their position. The usual missing ingredient was something inaccessible to conscious reason and hence unavailable for rational discourse. They often insisted that they just knew. I have tried to demonstrate that moral dilemmas are rarely struggles over making the best decision, but rather are implicit, stealthlike intrusions into the decision-making process. Only when everything that can be made explicit is openly considered can one hope to make a just claim for right or wrong.

Among pragmatism's (Goldberg 2002) essential ideas is the claim that decisions are not made by reference to a fixed standard but rather are created and recreated according to our history and experiences. This idea asks us to abandon our "myth of certainty" and to recognize that there are often many answers to a problem. Thus, the student who "knew" what was right and what was wrong is being honest to his or her personal set of judgments, all the while yearning for some absolute standard of conduct.

Pragmatism would caution Harvey Cox that often there is no absolute correct answer, and thus many moral struggles cannot possibly nor should not reach a happy solution for all times. Once these struggles are cleared of unconscious factors and seen primarily as a matter of rational choice, we may be able to better understand how dilemmas are resolved. We need to recognize that we are fundamentally only engaged in conversations which are aimed at increasing our capacities to better make our way in the world. Our vocabularies create our conceptual norms, and, inasmuch as we make our vocabularies, we also make our world and the truths about our world. Those of us with similar ways of speaking and conversing also see the world similarly. Of course, the commonality of vocabulary does not mean that we all speak English or any other communal language, but that our words share meaning. Thus, a simple word such as *patient* has to mean the same to me as to my colleagues. Since our vocabularies construct sentences and so concepts, we also share similar ideas and ways of thinking. We can only claim validity for what we do by being like-minded persons who constitute a community of support. A patient must have the same meaning to all of us.

The move by some from patient to friend or from patient to spouse is an opportunity to examine such a shift in status as being an act of social construction rather than of moral indiscretion. My discomfort with my ex-patient who wished to see me as both therapist and lunch companion, as I described earlier, was due to my personal inability to satisfactorily deal with this role ambiguity. My unhappiness with the psychiatrist who married his ex-patient was a similar form of category confusion that I experienced. How could someone who was clearly identified as a patient become transmogrified into a nonpatient? Of course, certain objects of the world are said to be essential and unchangeable (Mayr 1982). We all know what a triangle is, and it does not vary at all from one community to another. It is fixed. But, as we saw in chapter 11, a good deal of ambiguity inhabits our ideas about other issues, especially those dealing with obligations. Much of our language is subject to modification as it changes in its very use depending on the context of the situation and the meanings given to it by its users.

Patient and therapist bear a certain relationship to each other, which can be characterized in a number of ways. One dimension of this relationship is that of power, another that of knowledge, a third that of duties. No matter how one chooses to describe and delineate its features, they do not seem to comprise an egalitarian set of attributes or an interchangeable one. If one chooses to concentrate on any or all of these dimensions or any others, one can follow the conceptual change from patient to friend or lover. Each person may have an opinion about such a change or movement, and, as noted earlier, certain therapists and schools of therapy may differ mightily about such a move being major or minor, meaningless or even catastrophic. The therapist who espoused loving one's patient (chapter 4) would struggle less with such a move than the one who championed maximum self-control. What each of these therapists or schools of therapy has done is to modify the core concept of a patient. In sharp contrast with the essential nature of a triangle, the social construction of a patient is an enterprise of a community speaking the same language with the same meanings. For some communities, patients are friends. For others, they cannot be.

My personal unhappiness with the psychiatrist who married an ex-patient and the psychiatrist whose friends were mostly ex-patients seemed best explained as their no longer belonging to my community of analysts and therapists. We no longer shared the concept of patient and ex-patient, and the fact that it presented itself as a moral issue was but an example of how conceptual differences often become illuminated as moral struggles. Earlier I quoted Michael Oakeshott (1975, 78–79) to the effect that morality is not the voice of the divine but the voice of ourselves as members of a community. Moral judgments are practices in thinking, choosing, acting, and uttering. We may treat them as givens, and we may experience them as stealthlike or hidden or uncomfortable, but they, at bottom, are just the way we speak to one another.

Thus, my displeasure at those two was a recognition that they were alien to the community which we once had in common. My discomfort was in seeing them as speaking another tongue, and their defense was articulated in a language that I did not speak. I suppose they might claim that they showed moral courage in being steadfast in their beliefs. It is more likely that I could not comprehend their vernacular language, and so we seemed at odds with one another.

Many of these differences are negotiable or resolved by and in conversation, and this is why moral ambiguity should be welcomed as a way station to possible resolution. However, some differences seem unbridgeable. The varying concepts of what constitutes a patient may well be one example of a gap that discourse cannot span. Perhaps my unhappiness was a reaction to the loss of these individuals from the community, and perhaps their defense was a recognition of that gap and their inevitable alienation. The investigator who had his patients speak to a nonexistent therapist cannot possibly share the concept of a patient that most of us possess. It is when the issues that concern us carry us away from a previously shared concept of patienthood that we should become alert to a morality that claims to be foundational but is merely a temporary resting place, waiting for the next dilemma to intrude upon the scene.

REFERENCES

Abend, S. 2006. Article in press. *Psychoanalytic Quarterly*.

Alexander, F. [1958] 1964. Unexplored areas in psychoanalytic theory and treatment—Part II. In *The scope of psychoanalysis*, 319–25. New York: Basic Books.

Allen, B. 2000. Is it pragmatism? In Pettegrew 2000.

American Psychiatric Association. 2001. *The principles of medical ethics with annotations especially applicable to psychiatry*. 2001 edition (includes November 2003 amendments). Washington, DC: American Psychiatric Association.

American Psychoanalytic Association. 2004. Principles and standards of ethics for psychoanalysts. New York: American Psychoanalytic Association.

American Psychological Association. 2002. *Ethical principles of psychologists and code of conduct*. Washington, DC: American Psychological Association.

Applebaum, B. 2005. Interpretive neutrality. *Journal of the American Psychoanalytic Association* 53 (3):917–43.

Arlow, J. 1991. Conflict, trauma, and defeat. In *Conflict and compromise: Therapeutic implications*, ed. S. Dowling. Madison, CT: International Universities Press, p. 3–14.

Benedek, T. 1973. *Psychoanalytic investigations: Selected papers*. New York: Quadrangle.

Boesky, D. 2005. Psychoanalytic controversies contextualized. *Journal of the American Psychoanalytic Association* 33 (3):835–63.

Bollas, C., and D. Sundelsen. 1995. *The new informants*. Northvale, NJ: Jason Aronson, Inc.

Brenman Pick, I. 1985. Working through the countertransference. *International Journal of Psychoanalysis* 66:157–66.

Bridges, Nancy A. 2005. *Moving beyond the comfort zone in psychotherapy*. Lanham, NY: Jason Aronson.

Buber, M. 1961. *Between man and man*. Trans. R. G. Smith. London: Collins.

Bubner, R. 1981. *Modern German philosophy*. Cambridge: Cambridge Univ. Press.

Buechler, S. 2004. *Clinical values: Emotions that guide psychoanalytic treatment*. Hillsdale, NJ: Analytic Press.

Canestri, J. 1993. A cry of fire: Some considerations on transference love. In *On Freud's Observation on Transference Love*, ed. E. Person, A. Hazdlon, and P. Fonagy. New Haven, CT: Yale Univ. Press.

Caputo, J. 1997. *Deconstruction in a nutshell*. New York: Fordham Univ. Press, p. 137.

Churchland, P. 1989. *A neurocomputational perspective: The nature of mind and the structure of science*. Cambridge, MA: MIT Press.

Committee on Scientific Activities. 1984. Ethical conduct of research in psychoanalysis. *Bulletin of the American Psychoanalytic Association* 40:439–45.

Cox, H. 2004. *When Jesus came to Harvard*. Boston: Houghton Mifflin Co.

Dennett, D. 1991. *Consciousness explained*. Boston: Little, Brown & Co.

Derrida, J. 2002. Force of law: The "mystical foundation of authority." In *Acts of religion*, ed. Gil Anidjar. New York: Routledge.

Dewald, P. A., and R. W. Clark, eds. 2001. *Ethics case book of the American Psychoanalytic Association*. New York: American Psychoanalytic Association.

Dewey, J. [1934] 1991. *Art as experience in John Dewey: The later works*. Vol. 10, *1934*. Carbondale: Southern Illinois Univ. Press.

Edelstein, D. 2005. The ethic in ethics. *Illinois Psychiatric Society Mind Matters*, no. 9 (June): 10.

Eickhoff, F-W. 1993. A rereading of Freud's "Observations on transference love." In *On Freud's observations on transference love*, ed. E. Person, A. Hazelon, and P. Fonagy. New Haven, CT: Yale Univ. Press.

Fenichel, O. 1945. *The psychoanalytic theory of neurosis*. New York: W. W. Norton.

Flanagan, O. 1996. *Self expressions, mind, morals, and the meaning of life*. Oxford: Oxford Univ. Press.

———. 2000. *The problem of the soul*. New York: Basic Books.

Fonagy, P. 2001. *Attachment theory and psychoanalysis*. New York: Other Press.

Foucault, Michel. 1991. *Remarks on Marx: Conversations with Duccio Trombadori*. Trans. James Goldstein and James Cascaito. New York: Semiotext.

Frank, J. 1973. *Persuasion and healing: A comparative study of psychotherapy*. Rev. ed. Baltimore: Johns Hopkins Univ. Press.

Frawley-O'Dea, M. G., and J. E. Sarnat. 2001. *The supervisory relationship: A contemporary psychodynamic approach*. New York: Guilford Press.

Freeman, W. J. 2000. *How brains make up their minds*. New York: Columbia Univ. Press.

Freud, A. 1946. *The ego and the mechanisms of defense*. London: Imago.

Freud, S. [1895] 1953–74. Project for a scientific psychology. In *The standard edition of the complete psychological works of Sigmund Freud*, trans. under the general editorship of James Strachey with Anna Freud, assisted by Alix Strachey and Alan Tyson, 1:295–391. London: Hogarth Press.

———. [1912] 1953–74. Papers on technique. In *SE*, 12:115–16.

———. [1912] 1953–74. Recommendations to physicians practicing psychoanalysis. In *SE*, vol. 12.

———. [1915] 1953–74. Observations on transference love. In *SE*, vol. 12.

———. [1923] 1953–74. The ego and the id. In *SE*, 19:54.

———. [1926] 1953–74. Inhibitions, symptoms, and anxiety. In *SE*, vol. 21.

———. [1927] 1953–74. Humor. In *SE*, 21:159–66.

Gabbard, G. 2000. Disguise or consent: Problems and recommendations concerning the publication and presentation of clinical material. *International Journal of Psychoanalysis* 81:1071–83.

———. 2003. *Long term psychodynamic psychotherapy*. Washington, DC: American Psychiatric Press.

Galatzer-Levy, R. 2003. *Psychoanalytic research and confidentiality: Dilemmas in confidentiality, ethical perspectives, and clinical dilemmas*. Ed. C. Levin, A. Furlong, and M. K. O'Neill. Hillsdale, NJ: Analytic Press.

Gedo, J., and A. Goldberg. 1973. *Models of the mind: A psychoanalytic theory*. Chicago: Univ. of Chicago Press.

Glover, E. 1958. *The technique of psychoanalysis*. New York: International Universities Press.

Goldberg, A. 1999. *Being of two minds*. Hillsdale, NJ: Analytic Press.

———. 2001. Postmodern psychoanalysis. *International Journal of Psychoanalysis* 82 (1): 123–28.

———. 2002. American pragmatism and American psychoanalysis. *Psychoanalytic Quarterly* 71 (1): 235–250.

———. 2004. *Misunderstanding Freud*. New York: Other Press.

———. 2004. A risk of confidentiality. *International Journal of Psychoanalysis* 85, pt. 2: 301–10.

Gregory, I. 1979. Psychoanalysis, human nature, and human conduct. In *Nature and Conduct*, ed. R. S. Peters, 99–120. New York: St. Martin's Press.

Gutheil, T., and G. Gabbard. 1993. The concept of boundaries in clinical practice: Theoretical and risk-management dimensions. *American Journal of Psychiatry* 150:188–96.

Habermas, J. 1993. *Justification and application: Remarks on discourse ethics*. Trans. A. P. Cronin. Cambridge, MA: MIT Press.

———. 2003. *The future of human nature*. Cambridge, UK: Polity Press.

Hahn, L., ed. 1995. *The philosophy of Paul Ricoeur*. Chicago: Open Court.

Hand, S., ed. 1996. Martin Buber and the theory of knowledge. In *The Levinas Reader*. Oxford: Blackwell.

Harris, Roy. 2005. *The linguistics of history*. Edinburgh: Edinburgh Univ. Press.

Hartmann, H. 1939. *Ego psychology and the problem of adaptation*. New York: International Universities Press.

———. 1960. *Psychoanalysis and ethics*. New Haven, CT: Yale Univ. Press.

Harvard Ethics Consortium 2003. *Journal of Clinical Ethics* 19 (Spring–Summer): 88–133.

Hoffman, I. Z. 1994. Dialectical thinking and therapeutic action in the psychoanalytic process. *Psychoanalytic Quarterly* 63:187–218.

International Committee of Medical Journal Editors. 1995. Protection of patients' right to privacy. *British Medical Journal* 311 (7015): 1072.

Izard, C. E. 1977. *Human emotions*. NY: Plenum.

Jacobson, E. 1964. *The self and the object word*. New York: International Universities Press.

Jaffe, S. 2003. Public dialogues and the boundaries of moral community. *Journal of Clinical Ethics* 14 (12).

James, W. 1950. The consciousness of self. In *The principles of psychology*, chap. 10. New York: Dover Press.

Kant, I. [1781] 1965. *Critique of pure reason*. Trans. N. K. Smith. New York: St. Martin's Press.

Keats, John. [1817] 2001. Letter to his brothers. In *Complete poems and selected letters of John Keats*, 491–92. New York: Random House.

Kohlberg, L. 1984. *The psychology of moral development: The nature and validity of moral stages*. San Francisco: Harper & Row.

Kohut, H. 1971. *The analysis of the self*. New York: International Universities Press.

Lander, R. 2003. The incontinent analyst. *International Journal of Psychoanalysis* 84:891–95.

Lear, J. 2003. Confidentiality as a virtue. In *Confidentiality: Ethical perspectives and clinical dilemmas*, ed. C. Levin, A. Furlong, and M. O'Neil. Hillsdale, NJ: Analytic Press.

Levinas, E. 2001. *Is it righteous to be?* Ed. J. Robins. Stanford, CA: Stanford Univ. Press.

Lichtenberg, J., F. Lachmann, and J. Fosshage. 2002. *A spirit of inquiry: Communication in psychoanalysis*. Hillsdale, NJ: Analytic Press.

Lionells, M., J. Fisedline, C. H. Mann, and D. B. Stern, eds. 1995. *Handbook of interpersonal psychoanalysis.* Hillsdale, NJ: Analytic Press.

Litowitz, B. 2004. The origin of ethics: Deontic morality. *International Journal of Applied Psychoanalytic Studies* 2, no. 3 (2005): 249–59.

Lomas, P. 1990. *The limits of interpretation.* Northvale, NJ: Jason Aronson, Inc.

Mahler, M. 1975. *The psychological birth of the human infant: Separation and individuation.* New York: Perseus Books.

Maroda, K. 1999a. *Seduction, surrender and transformation.* Hillsdale, NJ: Analytic Press.

———. 1999b. Creating an intersubjective context for self-disclosure. Smith College Studies in Social Work 69 (2): 475–89.

Marsh, J. 2002. The right and the good. In *Ricoeur as another: The ethics of subjectivity*, ed. R. A. Cohen and J. L. Marsh. Albany: State Univ. of New York Press.

Mayr, E. 1982. *The growth of biological thought: Diversity, evolution, and inheritance.* Cambridge, MA: Harvard Univ. Press.

McDowell, J. 1994. *Mind and world.* Cambridge, MA: Harvard Univ. Press.

Mitchell, S. 1993. *Hope and dread in psychoanalysis.* New York: Basic Books.

Moore, B. E., and B. D. Fine. 1990. *Psychoanalytic terms and concepts.* New Haven, CT: Yale Univ. Press.

National Association of Social Workers. [1996] 1999. Code of ethics of the National Association of Social Workers. Revised by the 1999 NASW Delegate Assembly.

National Bioethics Advisory Committee. 1999. Research involving human biological material. Rockville, MD: US Department of Commerce.

Nehamas, A. 1985. *Nietzsche: Life as literature.* Cambridge, MA: Harvard Univ. Press.

Nietzsche, F. [1881] 1982. The dawn. In *The portable Nietzsche*, ed. and trans. W. Kaufman. New York: Penguin Books.

Oakeshott, M. 1975. *Of human conduct.* Oxford: Oxford Univ. Press.

Ornstein, A., and P. Ornstein. 2005. Conflict in contemporary work: A self psychological perspective. *Psychoanalytic Quarterly* 74 (1): 219–52.

Pettegrew, J., ed. 2000. *A pragmatist's progress.* Lanham, MD: Rowman & Littlefield.

Piaget, J. 1932. *The moral judgment of the child.* New York: Free Press.

Piers, G., and M. B. Singer. 1953. *Shame and guilt: A psychoanalytic and cultural study.* Springfield, IL: Thomas.

Putnam, H. 1999. *The threefold cord: Mind, body, and world.* New York: Columbia Univ. Press.

Quine, W. V. 1969. Epistemology naturalized. In *Ontological relativity and other essays.* New York: Columbia Univ. Press.

Ricoeur, P. 1970. *Freud and philosophy.* New Haven, CT: Yale Univ. Press.

Rorty, R. 1982. *Consequences of pragmatism.* Minneapolis: Univ. of Minnesota Press.

———. 1989. *Contingency, irony, and solidarity.* Cambridge: Cambridge Univ. Press.

Sandler, J., and L. Rosenblatt. 1962. The concept of the representational world. *Psychoanalytic Study of the Child* 17:128–48.

Schafer, R. 1976. *A new language for psychoanalysis.* New Haven, CT: Yale Univ. Press.

Searle, I. 1992. *The rediscovery of mind.* Cambridge, MA: MIT Press, Bradford Books.

Searles, H. 1965. Oedipal love in the countertransference. In *Collected papers on schizophrenia and related subjects*, ed. H. F. Searles, 284–303. New York: International Universities Press.

Shane, M., E. Shane, and M. Gales. 1997. *Intimate attachments: Toward a new self psychology.* New York: Guilford Press.

Slovenko, R. 1974. Psychotherapist-patient treatment privilege: A picture of misguided hope. *Catholic Univ. Law Review,* 23:650.

Stevenson, R. L. [1886] 2003. *The Strange Case of Dr. Jekyll and Mr. Hyde.* New York: Barnes and Noble.

Stoller, R. J. 1988. Patient's responses to their own case report. *Journal of the American Psychoanalytic Association* 36 (3): 371, 391.

Teicholz, J. 2000. The analyst's empathy, subjectivity, and authenticity: Affect as the common denominator. In *How responsive should we be? Progress in self psychology,* vol. 16, ed. A. Goldberg. Hillsdale, NJ: Analytic Press.

Thompson, M. G. 2004. *The ethic of honesty: The fundamental rule of psychoanalysis.* Amsterdam: Rodopi Press.

Tomkins, S. 1962–63. *Affect, imagery, consciousness.* Vols. 1 and 2. New York: Springer.

Wallwork, E. 1991. *Psychoanalysis and ethics.* New Haven, CT: Yale Univ. Press.

Williams, B. 1985. *Ethics and the limits of philosophy.* Cambridge, MA: Harvard Univ. Press.

Williams, M. 1999. *Groundless belief: An essay on the possibility of epistemology.* Princeton, NJ: Princeton Univ. Press.

Winnicott, D. 1954. Metapsychological and clinical aspects of regression within the psycho-analytic set-up. In *Collected Papers,* 278–91. New York: Basic Books.

Wolf, S. 1982. Moral saints. *Journal of Philosophy* 79, no. 8 (August): 349–439.

Žižek, S. 2004. A plea for ethical violence. *Umbr(a): A Journal of the Unconscious,* pp. 75–89. Buffalo, NY: Center for the Study of Psychoanalysis and Culture.

INDEX